# REFLECTIONS
# ON YACHTS

# REFLECTIONS ON YACHTS

*by*

## DOUGLAS PHILLIPS-BIRT
*Argus of the YACHTING MONTHLY*

## NAUTICAL PUBLISHING COMPANY
K. ADLARD COLES, COMMANDER ERROLL BRUCE R.N., Rtd.
*Captains Row, Lymington, Hampshire*

*in association with*
### GEORGE G. HARRAP & COMPANY LTD
*London Toronto Wellington Sydney*

© 1968 by D. Phillips-Birt

SBN 245 59567 8

*First published in Great Britain 1968
by* NAUTICAL PUBLISHING COMPANY
*Captains Row, Lymington, Hampshire, England*

*Composed in 12 on 13 pt Monotype Bembo and made and printed
in Great Britain by
Cox & Wyman Ltd., London, Fakenham and Reading*

# ACKNOWLEDGEMENTS

The author is indebted above all to the designers and builders of yachts. Also to the many people who during the last fifteen years have been interested enough in the ways of yachts to enliven the columns in which *Reflections* originally appeared, or who have written personally. The work of the latter is preserved in the top drawer of my desk in a file entitled Dewdrops and Brick-bats.

COMPANION VOLUME

Reflections in the Sea

*Also by the same author*

The Waters of Wight

Ships and Boat - The Nature of their Design

The Yachtsman's Weekend Book

Sailing Yacht Design

Motor Yacht and Boat Design

Finding Out About About the Vikings

Finding Out About the Phoenicians, Etc.

# PREFACE

In February 1952 I was given by Maurice Griffiths, Editor of the *Yachting Monthly* from 1926 to 1967, the hospitality of a monthly column under the title of *Reflections in the Sea*. It has always been precisely what the title implies – a title, incidentally, that owes something to Conrad's *Mirror of the Sea* and something to the essays of Charles Morgan, *Reflections in a Mirror*.

Although any working author having to supply the regular copy knows sometimes the passing boredom of the task in hand – like any worker in any other field – I have never been able to think of more pleasant work than to write about what one finds most interesting and fascinating, as a regular and modestly paid activity. From 1952 until the moment *Reflections* has been a happily accepted taskmaster. A writer having a subject and a pen, and with an editor who provides a regular platform, has been singularly blessed.

One has, however modest, to assume that the security of the platform depends on pleasing, 'for if you do not please you are not heard at all'. You get the sack, in fact. But a writer, if he wishes to survive, must never write just with the idea of pleasing the readers. He will write as well as he can only when satisfying himself. If, in the process, he pleases some kind of public, he secures some sort of platform.

Since *Reflections* has survived for sixteen years, they must have pleased a sufficiency of readers. To them, like my editors, former and present – I am grateful.

Now the publisher who brought out my first book is producing my latest under the imprint of his new firm, a selection made from the *Reflections* during these sixteen years together with a few additional pieces. Out of some 250,000 words about one-third has been winnowed to produce two companion volumes, of which this one is about yachts and yachting.

D. Phillips-Birt,
Royal Ocean Racing Club,
1968

# CONTENTS

# CONTENTS

# ILLUSTRATIONS

# I

# AS WE WERE

## AN EARLY YACHTING TRAGEDY

History is enlightenment – or can be. Certainly the history of yachting has high possibilities in this respect; for however far we reach into the past we find boats not unrecognizably different from those we know, and for ever on the shores of far-off days beats the same old sea. History, however, can make formidable reading – of this sort: 'Yeagh, yoath, yolke, yuaght, yaugh, yach, yackh, yought, yaught, jacht . . .' and then just as we are beginning to despair of ever seeing the light again: 'Yatcht, yat, yott,' and finally with a flourish the sun comes out and we read 'yacht'. We have learned, for the good of our souls, the many different ways in which the word 'yacht' has been spelt during its long story. But it is all rather dull. Perhaps it is the sort of history which Mr Ford once called bunk.

Long ago, in the days before yachts were called by any of these names, and when the map of Europe had names on it like Aquitaine, Navarre, and Anjou, there was a yachting tragedy. The vessel was La Blanche Nef, a white craft of fifty oars. She belonged to Henry II, the king who upset the powerful clerics of his day by chatting and doodling during their sermons. It happened late in the evening on November 25, 1120. The English king and his court were returning from Normandy, which like much of France at that time, belonged to him. The king left Barfleur, and La Blanche Nef, in which his son Prince William was to sail, prepared to follow. She had on board numerous of the young prince's friends, and also two of Henry's illegitimate children, Richard and Mary Countess of Perche. It was a gay party, and the gaiety was extended to the crew, who were well treated to wine before sailing.

So, on that distant, quiet November evening the glamour of the English and Norman nobility, no doubt twittering sophisticatedly in the style of A.D. 1120 and humming snatches of the madrigal of the moment, boarded the white yacht with their boy friends and put to sea. The crew pulled strongly hoping to overtake the King's ship. But the vessel suddenly struck a rock and foundered quickly, leaving only one survivor.

That was more than eight hundred years ago. Why retell this old and famous story? Not to point a moral I do assure you. Pointing morals is an immoral practice fraught with all uncharitableness. No. It simply happens to be a story having peculiar tragic charm to me – the still evening, the gaiety, the sudden disaster. Most people enjoy a well-constructed tragedy provided it is one of long ago or far away. And the fact that the King never smiled again is the final, perfect touch. History probably lies in this instance; but with what a perfect sense of style it does so.

## THE EMPRESS YACHTING

Ninety-five years ago the royal yacht *Victoria and Albert II* was loaned to the Empress of Austria for a cruise to Madeira. This vessel was an elegant paddle steamer with a fairly expansive schooner rig, built in 1855, and she served Queen Victoria for fifty years of her reign. There are several black-and-white wash drawings of the yacht by Wyllie in the National Maritime Museum, Greenwich, and also a coloured lithograph, and at Windsor Castle there is a water-colour of her by Sir Oswald Brierly.

The yacht had a reputation as a seaworthy vessel, but the letter of one of the Empress's attendants on reaching Madeira suggests the awe that a rough crossing of the Bay of Biscay may raise in a mind unversed in the habits of the sea. All was well for a few hours, but '. . . about three in the afternoon there arose a strong wind which made the ship rock . . .' and '. . . as darkness drew on, we were scarcely settled in our cabins, when we all became so ill and prostrate, that the good people in the ship knew not to whom first to give aid'.

The yacht's doctor, we are told, had no rest day or night; and then, just as they were beginning to think that the worst was over

'. . . the storm rose with such violence that even some of the officers and crew were ill; from this moment no imagination can picture how terrible it was; the ship groaned and cracked in her innermost parts, she rose and tossed about and struggled with the furious waves, but when we reached the insidious Bay of Biscay, it seemed as if all the evil water sprites had combined with the elements to destroy us. Our yacht is provided with the strongest machinery that this kind of vessel can have, and she likewise sails quickly; instead of sailing like we had done for two days before, 13 or 14 miles per hour, we only made the small progress of 4 miles an hour the whole of that day; our vessel strove boldly to advance, but a large mountain wave sent her reeling back'.

With the Empress affairs were little better, everything about her was scattered, '. . . nothing escaped in her Majesty's cabin nor in ours – the most necessary and useful utensils broken into a thousand pieces'. In these circumstances it is easy to understand that 'all was clatter and confusion' but as if this was not enough '. . . the terror of the people rose to the highest pitch, for the sailors fell from the masts . . .' though apparently only sprains and broken legs resulted. And thoughout '. . . The self-possession and composure of the captain was admirable and marvellous. . . .'

So this remote, foreign lady wrote ninety-five years ago from Funchal in Madeira, glancing up every occasionally towards the distant horizon and 'at the heavens stretching over my beloved Austria'.

## ABOUT A CENTURY AGO

'*Plus ca change plus c'est le meme chose.*' Or is it? One may wonder at times. After all, it was once the firm conviction of professional hands, and supported by the yachtsmen themselves, that the amateur was not capable of managing a yacht of any size. He might take the wheel occasionally, with that same expression of bewilderment which we see looking at us from the pages of the glossy weeklies where the racehorse owner is shown leading his winner back to the paddock; or toy with his sextant to see if his

answer resembled the skipper's! or even say where the yacht
should go, subject to the skipper's approval. But a gentleman was
not expected to know the seaman's trade. Naturally!

And naturally people agreed. It really was not an unreasonable
opinion, and we should all doubtless have acquiesced in it during
those days; sitting well-dressed, Victorian, and full of puns, in
a deck-chair beneath an awning, watching the nautical activity
around us and no more ashamed of not jumping up to turn a splice
in the nearest piece of rope than we should be of wearing a top
hat and racing glasses at Ascot instead of being on a horse's
back.

But even a century ago there were, apparently, those who felt
that yachting might be becoming a shade too decorative. There
were complaints about the '. . . struting and lolling about on deck
in blue pilot-cloth jackets with gilt buttons' at regattas, and about
telescopes being raised '. . . penetrating the throng of spectators,
and resting on the face of some fair, animated beauty, whose reply
to the yachtsman's telescopic signal is a careless waving of a white
cambric burgee, or a more pleasing response of kissing delicate
white hands . . . all of which may create very delightful sensations
. . . and is very, yes, *very* excusable . . . But couple not the name
of *yachtsman* with such delicate white hands . . .'

And so on. There is yards of it, all between the blue musty
cover's of *Hunt's Yachting Magazine* for a hundred summers ago.
Bless 'em; faced with such seamanlike feelings combined with sentiment, one can believe that yachtsmen have not changed one bit –
either this way *or* that. Yet one then turns over to find one of
those interminable serial stories (and why is there no yachting
fiction today?) all about villainous Baronets and the most en-
chanting sailing Peers, and of the darkest deeds perpetrated amongst
the moorings on dirty nights in Cowes Roads. What storms there
were then; what gossamer traceries of rigging swaying against a
background of torn skies; what passions, suppressed with such
beautiful good breeding, in panelled saloons where stewards slid
in and out like pats of hot butter; and what blue, blue blood everywhere, even more than there was salt, salt sea.

And today yachtsmen want for their reading only plebeian

facts, tabulated data from the polytechnic. We must all be suffering from Noel Coward's Twentieth Century Blues. Certainly there is change here.

One may read too the Veteran Yachtsman advising, a century ago, the young owner not to employ as his skipper one of that 'vulgar, illiterate class' who would be liable to steer the yacht in his shirt sleeves and with a pipe in his mouth. Furthermore, washing should not be hung by the crew from 'improper places', one of the improper places being from bowsprit shrouds; while the disgraceful exhibition of hanging shirts to dry on *Sunday* should be checked instantly. Lastly, said the Veteran, 'keep the crew at a respectable and respectful' distance. And don't use nautical terms to them. You will only get them wrong and make them laugh at you.

'. . . *plus c'est meme chose.*' Oh, surely not . . . ?

\*     \*     \*

A hundred springs ago Palmerston was being the terror of foreigners and the most popular member of the Cabinet; Disraeli had not yet started writing his lover-like letters to Queen Victoria; and Florence Nightingale had never seen the Crimea. A boisterous spring was the prelude to a boisterous summer, and in this month of March exactly a century ago a fleet of yachts opened the season by sailing from Blackwall to Erith through a snowstorm.

Later, early in May, the Royal Thames Yacht Club held its first race, for which a prize of £100 was given; which compares favourably, at nineteenth-century values, with the £20 nowadays offered to the winner in the Big-Class during Cowes Week. But at that time it was not uncommon for a yacht to win more than £1,000 in prizes during a season.

A visiting American yacht, the *Truant*, won the Royal Thames race by 23 minutes. She was a beamy centreboard boat, and English yachtsmen were rather bitter about her easy victory, objecting to her 'sliding keel' (the Royal Yacht Squadron banned such contraptions a year later) and calling the yacht – as English yachtsmen

have described American racing yachts for the last hundred years –
a *machine*.

The summer months blew by the big programme of Thames
racing being carried out mainly in rainstorms whilst the Royal
Harwich Regatta was spoilt by the weather and the absence of
many yachts which were weatherbound elsewhere. But there was
some racing at Harwich, and a brief study of it suggests that though
the Income-tax and the Empire may not now be what they were
then, neither fortunately is the handicapping. The 25-ton *Gossamer*
was due to race without time allowance against the colossal
Swedish schooner *Sverige* of 280 tons; but *Gossamer's* owner,
being apparently an advanced thinker, decided that the competition was unfair and withdrew. This, however, did not prevent the
Royal Yorkshire Yacht Club later in the season racing five yachts
against the *Sverige*, whose combined tonnage was only three-
quarters of their big sister's.

Another American yacht, the *Sylvie*, appeared for the Squadron
regatta in the Solent with a challenge to anything in Europe for
money or the honour of the Stars and Stripes. To the intense delight of the Solent she was only second in the race for the Squadron
Cup, being beaten by Mr William Peareth's *Julia*.

## THE ALBUM

We had once, in the employment of my family, a ship's husband;
a Welshman who had, I now do not doubt, his fair share of Celtic
failings; but one who was to me then the embodiment of all per-
fections. One day he spent a long time bent over a garden table
working with an indiarubber on a large, blue book. Shortly afterwards he gave me the book. It was an album of cuttings from the
yachting papers, which he had collected thirty years earlier. It is
in front of me as I write – now half a century old.

The first photograph sets the period. 'War and Peace' is its
caption, for it was taken in stirring days when the old order seemed
to be breaking up, when the solid earth seemed to tremble beneath the foot, when, in fact, the Boer War was in progress on
May 25, 1900. In the photograph we see, beneath the sky that

distant summer, H.M. transport *Kildonan Castle* leaving for Table Bay with '2,289 officers and men for service at the front'. A few cables off on her beam is the yawl *Brynhild*, at that moment the leading boat in the New Thames Yacht Club Handicap race. There was not much wind on that morning in the first May of the century – fifty-four Mays ago. *Brynhild* is running free; her spinnaker, her jib and jib-topsail hang in folds; her mainsheet droops in a bight; only her mizen and mizen staysail are pulling very gently; no more than just enough to give her steerage-way.

From the calms of fifty-four years ago we pass to the fresh winds of fifty-three years ago, and a picture of *Valkyrie*. She is close reaching with a jackyard topsail set. A flame of wind has come licking off the shore to windward laying her over until her great mainboom has struck the water, so that her lee bow wave's smother of foam is matched, farther aft, by another smother from this huge spar dragging through the sea.

Over the page there is another study of *Valkyrie*, under better control this time, beating to windward along the familiar Island shore, the Royal Yacht Squadron just disappearing behind her mizen. For she has become a yawl since last season, encouraged by the YRA handicapping system. The mainboom is shorter, and she carries a bumpkin over her long counter. The topmast is housed, and the yacht gives a fine impression of snugness and strength. She is sailing fast in the broken water, which the wind is whipping into feathery spray. Her deck is wet; but her angle of heel is moderate.

Next we come to *Satanita*, and she too, known to history as a cutter, is now a yawl. Her racing flag is aloft, she is well heeled, and our view, from low on the weather bow, reveals what no man will probably ever again see in the flesh on board a yacht – twenty head of crew appearing above the rail.

On the next page, in a small picture stuck in as an afterthought to fill the space at the corner, we are in 1900 again – at Cowes during the Week. Cowes, with all its present democratic glory of numbers, will be a shadow, in this fifty-fourth year of the century, of the pageant that it was in the first year. No *Valkyries*, no *Satanitas*, and above all no minstrels. But there they are, in the album, on Cowes Parade with a panorama of moored yachts spread behind them, on this August day when the century is young and hopeful in spite of the ominous rumbling of a far-away war. There they are, one playing a harp, another a fiddle, the third a flute, while the fourth is turning somersaults in the air. He is, at this moment, upside down, his feet pointing the way to heaven. The fifth has his feet on earth. He is making the collection.

## THEY HAVE ALWAYS BEEN WITH US

It is too often believed today that racing in very small craft is a product of modern yachting, and that in the days when yachting was grand – in the sense that the largest yachts were by today's standards enormous, and pretty numerous, too – it was only an eccentric fringe that did their racing in small craft or dinghies. But consider this:

'. . . during the summer months, in the bright evenings, from every coast village may be seen a fleet of little vessels flitting along the shore in the smooth water, and lying over to the land wind, which, in good weather, rises as the sun sets. Many of these boats are racing craft. and as each principal watering place has its club, there is no lack of sport on the Saturday afternoons, there being always one, sometimes two or three matches for the little ships.'

This might be a description of any tolerable part of the European (or indeed American) coast today. It is actually a description of the Firth of Clyde in the 1880s. The craft concerned were open boats generally of four sizes, 15 ft, 17 ft, 19 ft, and 22 ft overall.

About where is this written do you think – and when?

'. . . a new sport has been born – the racing of small yachts . . . the very perfection to which racing has been brought (in large yachts) tells in the same direction, because few men can afford to build large racers year by year to replace those that are outclassed. Yacht clubs have increased both in numbers and wealth, and the executives find that racing brings grist to the mill and repays the cost and the trouble. This especially applies to small yacht races. . . . Owners are not slow to avail themselves of the sport that offers, which on trial proves to possess many advantages over large yacht racing.' This might have been a description of the situation twenty years ago.

But it was the Solent, also in the 1880s. Two important classes involved were the 1-Raters and ½-Raters, which were very light skimming dishes with either centreboards or fin keels, ranging in length on the waterline respectively between 17 ft and 20 ft and 15 ft and 17 ft. In the season of 1892 the Solent clubs between them organized seventy-five races for the ½-Raters and sixty-four for the 1-Raters, which works out for each class at four or more races per week.

There was, of course, regular mid-week racing then for a four-month season. This is a scale of activity transcending anything known today in any of the numerous small classes, except, of course, in the numbers of boats involved. But the mere multi-tudinousness of an activity has no bearing upon its worth, except to the salesman. The well-known American yachting writer W. P. Stephens wrote, early in the present century, of this Solent scene:

'. . . a distinct class of small yachts came into general use in England in the eighties, increasing very rapidly. The Solent proved a healthy nursery for this infant fleet, and in time it almost rivalled the popularity of the large yachts. A special class of racing man came into existence, much time and money being devoted to designing, building and racing yachts of one-half, one, and two-and-one-half rating.'

It was while the Solent Rater was flourishing that the Bembridge Redwing appeared, half-decked keel boats, of shallow draft and 16 ft on the waterline. The class serves as the example of countless others, which during the last fifty to seventy years have provided local racing at ports around the coast. These have not gained the fame of the Redwings, partly because the latter belong to a fashionable Solent club, but chiefly because the Redwings, with their one-design hulls but rig unrestricted in all respects, except for a limit on actual area of 200 sq, ft, provided unique opportunities for experiments with sail plans. For forty years the original class, confined to the one club and harbour, provided as good and technically valuable class racing as any. Then a new design was produced in the mid-1930s which, now thirty years old, continues the Redwing story.

The crucial difference between today and yesterday has nothing to do with the moderns discovering a hitherto unrecognized world of pleasure and interest offered by small craft. Our great-grandfathers, rich or poor, knew this well. It has, where the small racing craft are concerned, nothing to do with the elaboration and refinement of the boats. The most sophisticated of such craft were refined and expensive eighty years ago.

The first outstanding difference, of course, is the enormously greater number of people now involved in sailing small boats; and this has nothing directly to do with yachting. It is just one aspect of the culminating population explosion reacting, in certain parts of the world, with prosperous societies.

For the moment only the Clyde and the Solent have been briefly considered. It should be appreciated that all round the coast in harbours and estuaries there were local classes of centreboard and small half-deck keel boats racing regularly. Some of the boats were of an economical type; but where racing pressures were high, their prices became comparable, in real cost, with the smart small boats of today. We should clear our minds of the idea that small racing craft used to be only the poor man's substitute for larger but economically out-of-reach vessels. Rich men in small boats have always been common on the racing stage. Racing in very large yachts has had a more chequered history than many people now appreciate. Various 'big classes' have gone switch-backing across the scene of the last and present century's yachting, diving into troughs of depression and rising to peaks of activity, usually for reasons quite trivial and indeed personal amongst small groups of owners. Racing in small boats, down to the smallest, has been steadily fashionable since the seventies and always common at suitable places on the coast. In numerous such places yacht clubs were founded in the last century, as Lloyd's Register will reveal, and their principal function was to organize local small-class racing for people living in the vicinity. And the essentially parochial character of much small-boat racing has not been totally submerged in the modern flood.

1. The cutter yacht 'Alarm' of 1830

*Science Museum*

2. Old Ryde Pier, circa 1830

3. Norris Castle, Isle of Wight, yacht, lugger and rowing boats, circa 1830

4. A famous photograph of a famous schooner – 'Suzanne'

*Photo: Beken*

Those boats that flecked the Clyde waters on Victorian summer evenings evolved from simple fishing-skiffs. They became more powerful and better canvassed. Clinker-built open boats with transom sterns and plumb ends, their era is most nakedly revealed to us in the fact that just above the turn of the bilge over the middle length there was a rack to take the movable ballast of shot bags (though not all clubs allowed movable ballast, when it had to go into the bottom), and crews were generally limited to three in the 17-ft and 19-ft boats to minimize the effect of live ballast. This brings us head-on with two now utterly discarded but once conventional Anglo-Saxon attitudes towards small open boats: (i) there was nothing objectional in their having fixed ballast; (ii) live ballast was slightly disreputable. Today these two attitudes are precisely reversed.

The boats were usually adapted for two rigs. One was a standing lug; the other a smaller lug on the mast stepped farther aft with a jib on a pretty long bowsprit; both rigs were of gigantic area to modern eyes, and with willowly swaying yards aloft. The combination of the rig and the ballasted hull might prejudice the boats in the eyes of the RYA. But a contemporary account says of them:

'Accidents of any kind are rare ... (none fatal) ... owing doubtless to the excellent rule enforced in all clubs that every boat shall carry life-saving apparatus to float every person on board.' That sounds quite modern, and suggests how slow progress has been, ninety years having been insufficient to decide on the most reliable form of personal buoyancy.

The best of these boats, it may be noted, were considered 'very expensive' by a contemporary in 1878 – a 19-ft boat would then have been £75, complete down to the three lifebelts at 15s. each; and adjusting to the scale of today's inflated currency, we must agree.

Those Solent raters, so much in vogue both inland and elsewhere on the coast, received the accolade of royal patronage when in 1893 the Queen presented a 50 Guineas Challenge Cup to be raced for annually by the Upper Thames Sailing Clubs. So far as the hulls were concerned the numerous ½-, 1- and 1½-Raters, which were so numerous and widespread during the '80s, '90s, and during the first decade of the present century, had hulls that would be perfectly acceptable today for any small keel-boat class. Indeed, we might remember with suitable awe that much the most numerous and widely spread of the present International keel-boat classes, the Star, was on Francis Sweisguth's drawing-board in William Gardner's design office at a time contemporary with the raters. The Star class was established in 1911. Its bulbed fin keel and chine hull has remained basically unaltered ever since, and though its rig has been lifted on several occasions, the present Bermudan version is, as it happens, surprisingly similar in proportions to the Bermudan rig carried by the American ½-Rater *Ethelwynn* in 1896. We have to remember, too, that the International Snipes, still amongst the largest dinghy classes, are venerable and rather heavy chine boats to a design thirty-years old.

In the Solent rater classes during their closely competitive days there was a small body of architects whose names were linked with the design of small racing craft – Ridsdale, Payne, Clayton, Feltham, Sibbick – together with the internationally known architects of large yachts, who found themselves competing in the 1- and ½-Raters classes, such as Soper, Fife, and the dominating American giant Herreshoff, and Charles E. Nicholson, then early in his career. The 1-Raters are still with us today in the Thames A Class, now carrying lofty Bermudan rigs and varying in waterline length between 15 ft 9 in. and 19 ft. These boats represent a class survival of eighty years.

We may have to remind ourselves today that the fame of many local classes, apart from the Redwing, was widespread in the world of yachting. The Water Wags of Dublin Bay, introduced in 1887, were originally described as 'an inexpensive unballasted centreboard sailing boat'. The boats, 14 ft 3 in. in length, 5 ft 3 in. beam, not only became widely known in their early years, when the character of their design was something of a novelty, but their fame has continued, along with their activity, in Dublin Bay (also, I believe, at a number of clubs in the Indian Ocean) while the many contemporary big racing classes of their days have passed by and been forgotten, or been remembered only for a few individual yachts of distinction out of their ranks.

The Water Wags are the oldest one-design class in the world – the Rater classes being designed to formula – and it seems peculiarly significant today that the class with this distinction should be one of unballasted racing dinghies.

The Water Wag story is similar to that of many dinghy classes since. The construction of the boats was at first inadequately covered by the drawings and specification – now eighty years later rules of integral calculus complexity liable to drive measurers 'stark staring bonkers', remedy this deficiency – and the popularity of the Water Wags resulted in the original price of the boats rising from £15 to £28; an increase of 90 per cent in a few years, which shows that racing dinghy developments could be as brisk in the 1880s as the 1960s. The latter amount was a considerable sum to pay in the 1880s for a 14-ft clinker-built open boat with a standing lug rig. So the Wags were redesigned to a tighter specification; the rig became a well-proportioned gunter sloop; planking had to be of the then cheap yellow pine instead of the cedar that had appeared in some earlier boats; and refinements of finish, such as fining the outside lands of the planks or bevelling the corners of the timbers, were outlawed. A modified design and specification was introduced in 1900; and then the class marched on into the revolutionary twentieth century, where it remains unembarrassed by the years.

The contemporary racing dinghy, and boats slightly larger exemplified in their most advanced form by the Tempest, have revolutionized small-boat sailing, but have left significantly untouched tastes in boats just a little larger. Even the sophisticated Solent has to offer three active, decidedly elderly classes – the X Class, Yarmouth One Design, and Victorys. Three classes, of which the X is the most numerous, are remarkably similar. They range between 16 ft and 18 ft on the waterline; 20 ft and 21 ft overall; they have 2 ft 6 in.–2 ft 9 in. of designed draught; they are half-decked; they are, in terms of the human being, quite-nicely-thank-you middled-aged.

Such as these or slightly smaller classes, unmistakably not dinghies though they may have centreboards, are scattered richly round the coast, and a characteristic of many amongst them is their

longevity – at least of their hulls: their rigs may have been modified. The names of designers of these boats sometimes appear like
a Victorian roll call, or at least a recital of the distinguished dead –
Linton Hope, Norman Dallimore, Alfred Mylne, G. V. Laws,
A. Westmacott. Local classes of long standing usually received
little publicity; which is no reflection upon them. Usually designed
to suit the special features of their own localities, like the old
working craft under sail, of which almost every port or open
roadstead round the coast had its own peculiar versions, such
classes usually achieved this ideal extremely well, and even the rolling by of a few generations does not affect their natural affinity
with their home port. As we have seen, even in the International
classes, where Stars and Snipes continue to satisfy numerous expert
sailors, small one-design or restricted-class sailing-craft are able to
elude *anno Domini* better than the human being.

Of course, there may come the time when a local class is composed mainly of over-elderly craft. A new type is considered. In
the past this would certainly have entailed going to an architect,
probably with good practical knowledge of local conditions, and
then presenting the plans and specifications to a local builder. Now
there is the alternative, supplied by various architects working in
collaboration with builders using line production methods, of
choosing what may seem a suitable class boat from the general
market, probably constructed in ply or plastics. The streamlining
of production may, at the present rate for shipwrights' work, reduce the initial cost of the boat, and also increase its investment
value by the extension, with any luck, of the second-hand market to
other fleets. This stereotyping has no other apparent advantage;
for such boats as these, which cannot be trailed or sailed to other
than closely neighbouring ports for racing, are essentially tied to
their home waters.

The one fundamental change in the dinghy and small-boat racing
world that has occurred over all this long period is the planing or
semi-planing ability, now regarded as essential in any dinghy class
likely to be of the slightest interest to the majority; and some form
of planing action is now expected in certain keel boats. Thus the
Flying Fifteen is as close as a kiss to the $\frac{1}{2}$-Raters of the '90s, except

only for having an adjustment in the run aft of the hull form that encourages a degree of dynamic lift. And even this feature was at least tentative in the Herreshoff ½-Rater *Wee Winn* and the Soper ½-Rater *Daisy* and many others in the '90s.

The planing action now taken for granted in dinghies has produced a profound break with the past. Before dinghies were called dinghies, but were referred to as sailing-boats, they were essentially of the big-craft breed though small in size. The 14-ft dinghy, for example, had something of the action of the bigger ship. Her centreboard was a fine heavy piece of iron; her buoyancy was in hefty brass tanks; there were side benches to sit on; an anchor and warp was up forward; and like the little ships they were, they lay at mooring. There are still classes of racing dinghy like that, but ever fewer. It is not a criticism but an observation to say that some of the salt has gone out of dinghies, and the successful, enormous classes which so adequately supply today's needs have *not* always been with us. They are a new genre.

# 2

# BRAVE NEW YACHTING

## OURSELVES TODAY

The following is controversial and to most, perhaps secure in the framework of contemporary views, rather shocking. Its theme might be shortly expressed thus: unless yachting becomes less popular and its participants a little less earnestly intense in the competitive way, there is danger that nobody who loved the activity for what it had to offer ten years ago will give a damn about it in fifteen years to come.

All men, it has been said, kill the thing they love (one of the most sinister possibilities we face in life). Perhaps contemporary yachtsmen, and those who in the industry produce the means of yachting, and those who write about it too, are doing just this by degrees at the moment.

We can surely say today that if enthusiasm be yet further whipped up about the joys to be found afloat, an awe-insipring effort will have to be made to increase the facilities of our awkward, industrialized, tide-ridden coast if the advertised joys are not going to be smothered altogether. They are already breathing hard.

The happiest yachting countries in Europe – the Scandinavias where, I believe, a higher proportion of the people go afloat regularly than anywhere else, including Holland – are blessed with a tiny population in relation to their long length of easily navigated, lovely coastline, where in almost tideless waters boats are easily moored or secured to slips and pontoons, and dinghies may be pushed in with a fraction of the skill and muscle required in most British places. We have a coastline bulging with the pressure of population behind it, heavily industrialized, swept by tides, with a few pleasant outlets to salt water through which the sea-hungry are bursting, crushed and crushing, and cheered on by encouragement.

C

I am aware that this is not the popular way of regarding the situation. Those few hundred (or is it few thousand?) boats at the hair-raising starts of Round the Island races; those few thousand (or is it a few million?) additions to the dinghy classes are applauded as admirable. To the sociologist as much as to the seaman they are alarming.

From the former's point of view, of course, such events are one aspect of the population-explosion of recent generations, and visible no less, if less miserably, in Hamble's crowded moorings than in London's midday traffic. Weight of numbers is no more admirable in yachts and dinghies than in the children of a family. Twice the number of children is to be deplored unless it means twice the number of equally well-fed, well-dressed, well-educated, happy children. It seems to me that we are giving birth to yachtsmen today far beyond the nation's ability to support them.

To be progressive and expansive is the twentieth century's way of right-thinking. The businessman, on the purely practical and immediate level, can, of course, hardly be expected to base his hopes and policy on other than expanding production. To create demand and then supply it is the essence of his activity. The outstanding feature of the post-war years in yachting, far transcending any technical developments in design or handling, has been the production-explosion in yachting.

Look at the amazing variety and number of exhibits at the next International Boat Show. Calculate the total cost of all the stands in terms of rent, transport of exhibits, salaries, lodging involved, and it may impress you that the industry should have enough money in it to make it worth while for exhibitors to come back year after year. Yet in the long, as opposed to the short, view such prosperity may be self-destroying. Balloons blown up too carelessly end up by bursting.

A production-explosion in yachting has dangers unique to itself. The situation is not analogous, as I once heard suggested, to the expansion in the motor industry that occurred after the early days of cars. For a brief period motoring was a gay adventure, and the knights on wheels steered the new horseless carriages along the winding, empty country lanes with aunts Agatha and Ermintrude in the back clutching their rugs and veils. Time passed; motors became commonplace; eventually they became an essential element in the transport system. Ownership of a car became a necessity rather than a pleasure; the factories spawned; and now there are few who venture on the road other than for the purpose of getting from A to B. It is no longer better to travel than to arrive, and often when travelling one's brightest hope is to arrive at all.

But yachts in mid-twentieth-century Britain can never become like the yacht in mid-seventeenth-century Holland – or the car today – a purely utilitarian means of transport. Nobody travels under power or sail other than for what they hope will be the pleasure of travelling; and if the day comes, which seems to be approaching so fast, when the estuaries and waters washing the more salubrious parts of our coast – and this is where the majority of yachtsmen want to be, not way out on deep water – become a nerve-racking ordeal to move about in, then one more much-needed source of human peace and refreshment will have been destroyed through over-exploitation.

Far more important today than winning the America's Cup, the Bermuda race, or a few more medals in the Olympics; more important than inventing new rigs, or improving the design of equipment, are the activities of such bodies as the Solent Protection Society and those planning elaborate and effective marinas. The capital outlay involved in the latter will be enormous if they are to be large and numerous enough to cope with further expansion; a vast expense would be involved simply by easing the present situation. And apart from the technical problems set by such artificial docks in our tidal waters, there is the further difficulty of obtaining sites in the few suitable localities. Those more interested in preserving natural foreshore rather than providing amenities for yachtsmen inevitably do not favour marinas.

In one further way the continued expansion of the British yachting public may eventually become possible without spoiling the virtue of yachting, and that is by the opening up to the remoter parts of our own and foreign coastlines for week-end yachting by means of air-travel. To some, but only a small extent this is already happening. Every year air travel becomes cheaper and less dependent on the weather. Some of the hectically busy yachting centres of today originated through the facilities of rail and road travel. Others may in time appear, thanks to the aeroplane. Let us hope so. We need them. And we need them soon.

Though I readily become absorbed in the problems of yacht research, and have written much about them, I have moments of doubt about the frenzy of intellectual and physical dedication now being encouraged in the cause of winning America's Cups, Olympic Medals, or even ocean races. There is something neurotic about it. I have always had an aversion from the idea that the game is greater than the player. Other nations may professionalize sport. It is the trend of this dim, earnest century with its threnody of fear. And it is the reverse of gracious or happy living, to which it is the function of sport to make a contribution.

Once the fleet of the Royal Yacht Squadron used to put to sea in formation and perform a stately minuet of naval evolutions directed by signals from the flagship, and watched from the decks by the wives and sweethearts of the proud owners, whose nautical attainments were sometimes little more than the knowledge of how to adjust a telescope (you may recall the story of the owner who, when approached by his skipper and asked whether he would like to take the wheel, replied that he took nothing between meals – and he wasn't trying to be funny). Then on one occasion some owners disturbed the minuet by going in for a little private racing, and their misbehaviour was firmly dealt with in a circular. This was absurd; yet there was a vestige of soundness in the instincts of the Victorian gentlemen who issued it.

We who today stand at the opposite extreme from their opinion may be able to discern the underlying sense. Hilaire Belloc said that if you let racing into boat sailing you let in the devil. As a precise statement of general truth this is, of course, nonsense; but it was not that wise man's way to talk *pure* nonsense, and he spoke often with the voice of prophesy, which is always hard to understand. Times will continue to change, as they have, and the day will come when people find as ludicrous our growing idea that it is virtue for a person to spend all his spare summer hours, energies and activities (and many of his working hours too and perhaps far too much of his income) to the winning of a pot, as we find that of the Victorian gentlemen who disliked a little racing to enliven a tedious Solent afternoon.

These views are not purely Argusian. They are inspired by the comments of a once-well-known helmsman, who had the intelligence to notice the much higher standards of helmsmanship and handling evident amongst the best today than there used to be. 'But then,' he added, 'they seem to eat, drink and sleep the business today. It's the modern manner, I know. But when sport ceases to be amateur even amongst the amateurs, a change of attitude is approaching.'

The cult of over-efficiency in sport or games destroys what it seeks to improve. It produces in a short time the spectator sport or game, which is a different commodity altogether. Sport, like love, must have running through it a thread of the gay and spontaneous if it is to preserve its purity of purpose, which is to make the lives of people fuller and their hearts more generous.

\* \* \*

Nothing – but, I swear, *nothing* – so truly symbolizes the brave new yachting as that wonderful little Honeywell computer purring, gurgling and regurgitating tirelessly through the smiling hours of Cowes Week and providing quick as a flash, or quicker, those neat lists of results displayed outside the Regatta Centre.

Had some amazing human brain never devised the Series 200 Honeywell computer, I suppose Cowes Week would not have come to a standstill. *Deus ex machina* has often ruled the Cowes days, but without this new *machina* one feels that *Deus* would have had to carry altogether too crushing a load for there to be any hope of orderly progress through the programme. For it would be quite beyond the powers of ordinary race officers, who sometimes cannot even fire the guns when they should under present conditions.

I should make it clear the Honeywell is not at Cowes during the Week. Like a true scientist he disdains social ambition and stays a hundred-odd miles away at Brentwood. But his acolytes are continuously at work in the Telex Terminal of the Regatta Centre feeding him with sail numbers and yachts' times *a la* punched tape. On one side of the Telex Terminal Honeywell's creatures transmit the raw, crude information. On the other they receive neat lists of corrected times.

It will become better than this before long. The whole organization will be automated. No longer will the intense faces of race officers peer out from amongst the Squadron battlements like knights in a tight corner at Plassey. We shall just see a Honeywell with an expression as cool as a Zombie doing everything perfectly, and only the yachtsmen out on the water will make any mistakes.

## PLAYING THE GAME

Until a while ago I had never heard of Brian Close, and thought that Colin Cowdrey had to do with horses and not cricket (forgive me). Then the two names began cropping up continually in the local yacht club. The America's Cup passed by with hardly a mention of the names of Jock Sturrock or Bus Mosbacher; not so however test cricket and the matter of Mr Close, and in that royal and ancient institution I gained the impression that he was decidedly unpopular. I think I recognized too familiar initials beneath a decidedly rude letter about him in the *Daily Telegraph* correspondence columns. Evidently he was a 'bad-thing'; and then the MCC Committee came to the same conclusion.

Listening to the talk swinging to and fro, it seemed to me that while the subject matter was unfamiliar in detail, the broad issue was well-trodden. And it occurred to me that there is no body in contemporary yachting that could give effect to the attitude towards sport shown by the MCC Committee in dismissing Close from the captaincy. Such an old-fashioned sense of what is and what is not suitable in sport could hardly gain practical expression in contemporary, very expensive international yachting, which has been moving in the opposite direction for many years now.

A long time ago Billy was a ship's husband looking after a considerable fleet of trawlers for my grandfather and later my father. When not so engaged his interest was sailing and the grander yachting which he saw for himself only on holiday visits to the Solent. In later years he talked a lot to me about the America's Cup, about which he had collected a big album of press cuttings reaching back for decades, which is now by me. According to Billy, it was only dirty work by the Yanks that had stopped our regaining the cup time and time again. His opinion of our cousins across the water and our recent allies in the 1914–18 war was about on a level with that about the Germans, who had lately sunk several of 'his' trawlers. At that time my father had admonished me: 'You must not take too seriously what Billy says about the America's Cup. He does not look at sport quite as we do, splendid fellow though he is.' Which puzzled my young mind quite a lot. And I need hardly say that my father keenly supports the MCC's recent decision.

The attitude that it represents has little place in the bigger international yachting events today, whether it be an America's Cup contest, Olympic yachting or less publicized events involving, however, a considerable expenditure of money, or time, which now for most people is money in another shape, and concern so many people who, whatever their official status, are ethically professionals, from the designers and builders of the yachts to the people who write about them. And when, on top of these powerful influences, we have modern nationalism, the grim competition between the De Gaulles of this world, whatever their ideology, reaching out over the tennis courts and the clean sea, quite clearly the relationship between the old and new ideas of sport is as remote as medieval jousting from modern war.

But the British have been slower to adopt the modern attitude than other nations, and international yachting shows many examples of what we may call the old and new ideas of playing the game in conflict. There is, however, a residue of generally accepted change. Could, for example, this happen today: two yachts are involved in an America's Cup race. The defender grossly fouls the challenger under the rudimentary port and starboard rule and a collision follows, in which the former is put out of the race through damage. There is no argument about the interpretation

of the rule, and the challenger is told that if she sails round the
course the race is hers. The owner refuses to do so: 'I came for a
race not a sail over.' Thus Sir Richard Sutton, owner of *Genesta*,
in 1885. Could such an attitude be adopted with a syndicate-
owned, highly financed challenger, manned by a crew which has
sacrificed time and work and undergone a racking ritual of training, forsaking all and living laborious days?

The logic of the situation today is more likely to produce what
occurred half a century later. The challenger, at the crucial stage,
had won two races to the defender's one, and she was clearly the
better yacht though not so well handled. In the fourth of the races
the failure of the defender to respond to a luff by the challenger
(or so it seemed) allowed the former to slip into the lead and the
challenger protested. The protest flag was not hoisted until she
came within sight of the committee boat, which was approved by
the American official observer on board and in accordance with
the IYRU rules as they then were. The committee refused to hear
the protest on the grounds that a local rule laid down that the
protest flag must be hoisted immediately after the event. This
occurred in the races between *Endeavour* and *Rainbow* in 1934.
It was an unfortunate piece of legalism which was generally unpopular on both sides of the Atlantic, and led to headlines in a
New York newspaper 'Britannia rules the waves but America
waives the rules'. Which was not quite true. The committee inter-
preted the rules rigorously and possibly also saved the cup from
crossing the Atlantic. But perish the name of sport!

In any sailing contest, if the boats and the time involved represent in terms of money too great a sacrifice and responsiblity
the wrong spirit must enter; and if backers are concerned the
whole affair becomes involved in duties that are the antithesis of
sport. The delicate balance between a whole-hearted will to win
and over-enthusiasm to do so is easily upset. It is the old matter of
gentlemen v players, tolerance v efficiency, love of living v struggle
to live, and ultimately it is a matter of human acceptance v human
fear. Within its tiny limits of influence, the gentleman's ideal of
sport has a religious quality, which the old-fashioned gentlemen
who followed it would be the last people to appreciate. It had no

close relationship with that beastly little boy imagined by Sir
Henry Newbolt.

> 'The voice of a schoolboy rallies the ranks:
> "Play up! Play up! and play the game!"'

– little shocker! It was the luxurious ethic of the otherwise secure
adult. It depended upon an ethos unattainable in any sport followed
by millions which in turn follows the leaders of the modern rat
race, in which nobody is secure.

## VIVE LA FRANCE

We all admired Eric Tabarly of the French Navy for his victory
in the Singlehanded Transatlantic race. But I for one curl up at the
attitude to the victory expressed in *Paris Jour,* and I understand in
several other newspapers, at the time: 'Bravo, Tabarly. Thanks
to him it is the French flag which triumphs in the longest and
most spectacular race on that ocean which the Anglo-Saxons consider their special domain.'

That vacuous congratulation might have had a precursor had
some deep-blue traditional Yankee written in the New York
*Herald-Tribune* in 1928, when Paul Hammond's *Nina* gained the
first of so many American victories in the Fastnet race: 'Bravo,
Hammond. Thanks to him it is the American flag which triumphs
in the longest and most spectacular ocean race in those seas which
the goddam Britishers who loosed the *Alabama* on us consider
their special domain.'

How fortunate we are that the more conventional ocean racing
is still not conducted on the lines of rapturous nationalism and
ballyhoo that now characterizes sections of the Olympic Games
and Wimbledon; and as this attitude to a fine French seaman
indicates, it does not necessarily require the participation in
international sport of nations on the other side of that curtain
to produce idiocy.

Instantly President de Gaulle made Tabarly a Chevalier of the
Legion of Honour, and alas the *Daily Telegraph* decided to com-
pare favourable this brisk and ill-bred chauvinism with our own

attitude to Francis Chichester, who won the 1960 Singlehanded Transatlantic race and some while later received a C.B.E. It should have been given immediately, suggested the *Telegraph*.

It might be suggested that in the 1960 race all the competitors were British; also that Francis Chichester was a distinguished man in the world of aviation long before he took to singlehanded oceanic crossings, and that the former as much as the latter may have influenced his receiving the honour. There is surely a difference not of degree but of kind between this sort of delayed honour and one rushed out by a head of state in the heat of the competitive moment in a sport. May our Government never be inspired to dish out hot-footed honours in *international* sporting events.

International sport is a precarious enough structure without being further wobbled by that kind of enthusiasm. It is satisfying to think that when once it was suggested that an ocean race might form part of the Olympic Games the RORC turned down the idea as being inimical to the idea of the activity it sought to encourage.

It is a pleasure to return to the sanity of wise old Thomas Fleming Day: 'If man is a good sailor, I love him: I don't care whether he is black, white or yellow, what flag he sails under, or what God he kneels to.'

## OFFSHORE RACING MATTERS

We should first clear up a little nonsense about the inclusion of offshore racing in the Olympic Games of 1972. Now the Olympic Games once included a horse race and a chariot race, so I suppose there is nothing too far beyond the spirit of the affair to introduce an offshore yacht race; though, in fact, some people may see a distinction between chariots tearing round brief circuits during a sunny Peloponnesian afternoon, watched by enthusiastic crowds of the first people who called themselves democrats, and days spent racing out of sight of land watched by nobody at all, not even by twentieth-century totalitarians.

This, however, must be decided by those who know something about the spirit of the old Olympiads – *circa* 776 B.C. and later –

which we may hope was better than it is today. Before then, of course, Hercules was involved in the very earliest Games, of which no precise historical record now exists; but we can quite definitely say that never since Hercules have such foolish ideas been put forward as those of the International Yacht Racing Union lately, that there should be a sixth yachting class in the 1972 Olympic Games, that it should be for offshore racing, that the type of boat should be 'one of between 19 ft and 22 ft RORC rating, and furthermore (here it comes) that the Royal Ocean Racing Club and the Cruising Club of America and the Offshore Rules Co-ordinating Committee (ORCC) should *develop a common international measurement rule by November 1968*'. What a crescendo of odd, rising to idiotic, ideas!

By all means let the Olympic enthusiasts have an offshore race in the Games if they think it suitable; let them even be so preposterous as to have the boats designed to a rating rule if they like – the RORC with their celebrated Attic graciousness will no doubt lend theirs for the occasion, or any bits of it that may come in handy; but may Hercules preserve us from anything so mad as rushing up a special rating rule for the purpose. How many members of the RORC are there for whom the Olympic Games do other than bore the skylights out of them?

I should recall that immediately before the war there were suggestions that ocean racing should be included in the Games that were then due to take place in 1944. In *British Ocean Racing* (published by Adlard Coles Ltd) it is said: '. . . the idea did not gain much support and was emphatically condemned by the Commodore, Michael Mason, who pointed out that there were ample reasons for the RORC keeping out of any such race. Judging by the record of some other events run by the Olympic Games Association, there was danger of bad blood being stirred up between the countries concerned, in direct contrast to the policy of the RORC.'

*    *    *

Current ideas about evolving a common international rating rule are worthy of consideration, of course, quite apart from the

Olympic Games. There is a certain obvious tidiness and logic in them. But this does not mean they are such good ideas as they may seem to those who assume the role of leading, with something less than the sweet music of Hamelin's piper, the regiments of the uniform and tidy-minded towards the wondrous portals of a world where everything is the same everywhere (that death of the universe known to science as maximum entropy).

It is questionable whether a common rating rule for international use is either philosophically desirable or even practicable. We should not forget that there are three, not two established offshore rating rules already in existence; for apart from those of the RORC and CCA there is the International Yacht Racing Union's Cruiser-Racer rule, produced with all the mountainous labours of an international formulation – it was being said after the war, when it was in production, that its time of gestation was longer than that of an elephant – and its special object was to enable yachts to race together without time allowance as a class either round the buoys or offshore; or they might, as some of the boats have done, join the offshore fleet under RORC rating and time allowance.

The rule originally catered for various classes down to 7-Metres, of which the comely and conveniently sized 8-Metre class, coming out at 26½ ft–28 ft on the waterline, has alone gained any following. When the Cercle de la Voile de Paris put the One Cup back into circulation, it was presumably because there were a number of boats more or less of the appropriate size built to the RORC rule already in existence, that this rule was chosen for the event; with the further encouragement that further boats to so well-known and widely used a rule were more likely to find favour than ones to a little known class. Otherwise the IYRU C-R rule in the 7-Metre size would have been the obvious choice for the purpose of combined inshore and offshore events in boats of equal rating – *precisely* the purpose for which the IYRU Cruiser-Racer rules were devised. And why, if there is to be offshore Olympic racing in other than a One Design class of boat – the only rational system – this class should not be chosen, surpasses the understanding of those not endowed with the reasoning processes of the IYRU.

So far as the One Ton Cup was concerned, as we all know, the RORC rule was adopted with a fixed rating of 22 ft and to help it stand the pressure of fixed rating design some of the accommodational rules of the 8-Metre Cruiser-Racer class were added. The results, from the design point of view, have been probably much more interesting than anything that would have been produced had the Cruiser-Racer rules been adopted *in toto*: and more fun in this direction may be expected in the future.

Indeed, it is reasonably doubted whether the RORC rule will be able to withstand the competitive design to a fixed rating with out producing undesirable developments, and what we might call 'local stiffening' may be required; though the modifications to be made in the rule, which it is intended to make effective in 1970, may obviate this. But there is no reason why adjustments should not be made to suit One Ton and Half Ton cup boats alone. Such has been done before, by the JOG for example, and other bodies all over the world. There are, however, excellent reasons why a rule intended primarily to measure a wide range of yachts for rating under time allowance should not be distorted in its basic form to suit a limited number of fixed rating boats.

I have been unable to discover why a single international off-shore rating rule should be regarded as so desirable. But I had supposed, judging by what I had read and heard lately, that people at a certain RORC Press meeting would have been wringing their hands over yachtsmen from the farthest shore of the curtained-off Baltic to the sunlit harbours where the Pacific endlessly roars, who are in a state of helpless confusion for lack of a common rating rule. All that happened was that technical points were raised about improvements on rules, interesting but unconnected with the agenda.

In the early 1930s there was a missed opportunity of having a common rating rule on both sides of the Atlantic. That it was missed was not regretted by many also on both sides of the Atlantic. Again to quote from *British Ocean Racing*: 'For the mixed-type cruiser-racer fleets racing under handicap . . . separate rules are best able to cater for national tastes in yachts. Design is not

stereotyped, and much of value and interest is learned when the
yachts of two nations meet and race under the ratings and time
allowances of each other's rules. Furthermore, a rule once internationalized becomes harder to administer and control.'

This seems as true today as when it was written only six years
ago. Because class racing in a new guise, with an offshore racing
element in it, has now appeared, can anyone reasonably claim that
existing measurement rules should be internationalized and
dragooned in its cause? The sailing waters of the world are numerous and of great variety. Why exchange having the basic RORC
and CCA rules as twin norms in favour of the deadening uniformity
of a single rule intended, it appears, to cater for every locality,
for level and handicap racing, for inshore and offshore?

\*     \*     \*

A reasonably good yacht measurement rule is a delicate mechanism. Time was when a Dixon Kemp could get up and say: 'Right,
let's multiply the length on the waterline by the sail area, divide
the result by 6,000 to make a nice little nobbly number out of it,
which even the mathematically illiterate have learned to count up
to at school, and let's call the answer the yacht's rating.' He said
something like this in 1888; and like a garden under the kiss of
spring the rule flowered into *Britannia*, *Valkyrie*, *Calluna*, *Ailsa*
and a host of the fairest blooms.

But it was the Garden of Eden. Yacht architects such as George
L. Watson and Charles E. Nicholson ate of the tree of knowledge,
and all their clients and the sons of their clients down to the last
generation that could afford more than a punt found themselves
in a wilderness where ten times as many rules as the Decalogue
contains could only just prevent the architects from producing
monstrous growths. And so rating rules instead of looking like
this: LWL × Sail Area ÷ 6,000 = rating, became fat books of
small print having countless sub-paras., a concourse of tables and
equations each one more complicated than the whole of that naked
and innocent rule of 1888.

This is where we stand today.

A yacht measurement rule seeks to do something very difficult: to assess, as far as practicable, the factors that govern the performance of a sailing-yacht, and to combine them in a such way that a single number emerges at the end of the sum which is an index of the yacht's speed potential – her rating. Two yachts of the same rating are assumed to have the same speed potential. At the best this is no more than an approximation. First, sailing-yachts race in various strengths of wind, on various points of sailing; winds change in the course of a race; sometimes the sea is smooth, sometimes not. Even the perfect rating rule would apply perfectly only to one racing course in one set of weather conditions. Secondly, nobody has yet discovered how to combine the various speed factors so that each has precisely the right weight hydrodynamically even under idealized conditions. This is a problem in pure naval architecture, in hydrodynamics, an intellectual matter. The merit of any solutions to it is likely to be in the inverse proportion to the number of technically unequipped Charlies who are in a position to enforce silly ideas: such, for example, as that a new, common international rule might be produced by 'combining' the RORC and CCA rules; which is no less outrageous than supposing that we might blend 'God Save the Queen' with the 'Marseillaise' to produce an International Anthem for the Common Market. A fundamental trouble with an internationally controlled rule is the lack of cohesion in direction.

Then there is the administration of the rule. It should be emphasized that a rating rule needs constant revision involving modifications to arrest undesirable trends or to cater for new developments. This is the price that has to be paid for freedom of design. Many criticisms may be made of the RORC rules and its management. There are signs that the wood is not always seen for the trees for lack of the perspective given by sound basic theory. But it is governed by a private committee rocked by less confusion than an international committee drawn at inconvenient intervals from the corners of the earth for a party. And the rule is a more practicable one than the more boffin-controlled rule of the CCA.

## BOAT SHOWS

Boat shows effectively emphasize one characteristic of the contemporary yachting scene – the tremendously wide range of
choice open to the yachtsman in whatever it may be he wants,
from a motor-sailer to a mooring buoy. As I heard one person
saying to another: 'What a lot of people there are here all making
the same things.' The reply was : 'Well, that's what we want isn't
it – competition?'

And I do think that it is in regard to the boats themselves that
this aspect of the situation is peculiarly impressive and not what
casually we expect. We tend to have an impression today of boats
being produced in the mass, with dinghy classes running into
thousands of identical boats and even quite large craft, sail or
power, rarely being one-off creations but grouped into class-
types, sometimes almost one-design in nature, or at least basic
hulls. Amongst hundreds of these classes such well-known examples as the twelve-year-old South Coast One-Design, the
Fairey Fisherman, the Port Hamble Horizon class of 32-ft loa
motor-sailers, and the Camper & Nicholsons plastic sloops built
by Halmatic come to mind. Motor-sailers, indeed, now regularly
appear in classes and sell quite well in them. It is hardly too much
to say that every architect producing a design for a yacht of less
than 40 ft in length (and even more) is now liable to attach a class
name to it and trust that it will prolificate. So many architects
have now done this that I believe drawings producing one boat
only courts suspicion of being eccentric, if not a downright failure.

Which might appear to indicate that variety in design is becoming less than in the past. Yet in fact the reverse is so. The
multiplication of boats from common designs, tending towards
standardization, is at present offset by the huge market compared
with the past. All these groups of similar or identical boats are
derived from more individual designs and offer a great variety
of type than was available for the yachtsmen of the 'thirties to
choose from, though the majority of yachts other than class racing
boats were then one-off from individual designs.

Not only is the range of choice amongst yachts wider today than before the war, but the standards of design for boats lying in the size between dinghies and say 10 tons TM is much superior. Indeed, as late as the 'thirties, the average standard of cruising yachts in the 5-10 tons category was in general decidedly low – far lower than the existing knowledge of yacht design could excuse.

I should not like to sound any fatuous Panglossian note about all being for the best in the best of all possible worlds. But despite all the contemporary influences that discourage variety (or diversification, as a friend of mine might call it when adding weight by syllables) of which wood and plastics mouldings for hulls are the more powerful, and the reduction in costs that may be achieved by a degree of line production with orthodox timber construction is an important secondary influence, there is still today, whatever type of boat a yachtsman may want, a far bigger range of well-designed craft to choose from in the popular sizes.

Which is no doubt pretty distressing to the production-wise, efficiency-demented, time-and-motion-minded tycoon clamouring for massive combines and the streamlining of industry. No doubt the prices of boats and fittings could be materially reduced were Sir Max Efficiency and his fellow conspirator against human happiness, Lord Takeover (1st Baron), given a freer hand. Let us hope for a few years of relative inefficiency and lots of interestingly different boats from the yacht building industry.

Musing thus, strolling down Aisle N, suddenly I beheld in the middle distance the most (to me) beautiful boat in the Show. King Edward VII, I was realizing a few minutes later, had been on the throne when the hoary hands of Caledonian shipwrights, working as tenderly as gardeners planting basil, had bent those slender rock elm timbers and laid to those speaking curves the strakes of shell-like clinker planking in rich yellow pine. It was the stand of Alexander Robertson, and David Boyd was beside me crooning almost over this glorious piece of boatbuilding just 15 ft long and 4 ft wide, built as the yacht's gig for the steam yacht *Ariana* in 1902.

She was a naval gig in miniature; and this says enough for some people about the intrinsic harmony of her narrow, double-ended form – the splendid sweep of the gunwale in sheer from the proud

but unemphatic stem to the stern where the rudder head was
crowned by a brightly polished, gracefully wrought brass yoke;
and the other sweep of the gunwale in plan, with its fineness forward and then the bold curve round into the pointed yet buxom
stern with something Dutch about it. For the stern of a gig softens
the Viking severity of the basic form, and gives to this type of
boat a sophistication that the Thorberg Skaftings beside their
fjords never attained.

'You'd be surprised,' remarked David Boyd, 'how much attention she has caused.' I had become aware of this during a short
time on the stand. We were still cataloguing the virtues when
another person stopped and looked and felt and paused, and then
enunciated: 'Good t'thee lass, t'prettiest bint in Show.' Which,
I observed, was a hefty compliment to come from the Dales.

*         *         *

It seemed important to feed the squirrels. They came down the
trees at the lure of nuts and fanned around the outcrops of dark
green basalt rock, cracking the nuts with great refinement. Then
we went across the way to the 57th National Boat Show, in the
Coliseum just by Central Park.

Much that is in New York makes a European feel he has become less than life-size. But here at least everything seemed to be
on the familiar scale. True, there were more floors than at Earls
Court; but, surprisingly, there were fewer boats, and while there
was more space everywhere, there were no yachts of the size and
distinction of the more outstanding exhibits at the London show.
Nor was there the imagination and sense of style so apparent in
the arrangements and stage setting of the so much younger International Boat Show.

And there was no pool. A lot of idiotic things happen round that
pool with its stage set of architecture in the centre of the ground
floor at Earls Court, but most of them are rather fun; besides which
about a dozen most respectable yachts lie afloat in it. There is
nothing, after all, like introducing a little real water into a boat
show.

No, compressed into its smaller space, there is annually at Earls Court taste and atmosphere, a sense of theme and unity in the scheme, lacking at the Coliseum. And the boats exhibited are in the balance appreciably more interesting. Standing like Ruth amid the alien corn, I felt deeply stricken by those ranks upon ranks of plastic motor boats.

Could these be meet craft for the thousands of miles of America's wonder waterways? But at least it was amusing to see on some of the boats little grooves in the hull moulding in imitation of wood planking – fishing craft style, with nice showy seams. I, too, cultivate the antique.

But when one turned from boats to fittings and equipment, the story was different. The riches were scarcely credible. Here indeed was revealed the multiplicity of the New World compared with the paucity of the Old. Nowhere could be seen a more striking revelation of the change that has overtaken fore and aft sail since the days when the only mechnical appliances found on board would be the anchor winch or windlass, and possibly a roller reefing gear.

# 3

# THE YACHT HERSELF

## FAITHFUL OWNERSHIP

A habit once common and now almost unknown is that of keeping a yacht for many years and altering her extensively in the course of her long life. Yachts apparently do not live so long as they did. If this is indeed so it must be because people no longer seem to want them to live long rather than because they fall to pieces any sooner than was once usual. Sentiment, perhaps, is not the force that it used to be. At least it is rare now to find the strenuous efforts to keep an old ship alive that so many owners once made. Of such owners King George V was an outstanding example.

Between the spring afternoon of 1893 when *Britannia* fought her way through *Valkyrie II*, *Calluna*, and *Iverna* to her first victory, to the still midnight forty-three years later, when mastless and in tow of a destroyer she passed unwatched through the Needles and out into the Channel to be scuttled, she underwent numerous alterations. She had known seven major changes of rig. She had been converted into a cruiser, with high bulwarks and a deckhouse. She had been reconverted into a racer. She had had a length of 2,500 ft of hull planking renewed, including the replacement of the original cedar topsides by teak. Her ballasting had been altered and her keel profile modified. She had been re-sparred again and again.

Yet many examples may be found in the story of yachting which match that of this lovingly-tended royal yacht. There have been yachts which have lived longer and still retained a high place in racing. There have been those which have undergone even more extensive alterations. Throughout her career the shape of *Britannia* was carefully preserved. Yet a number of yachts in the past had almost every feature changed but the form of their midship section, ending their career with a fifty per cent higher tonnage than that with which they began it, rigged as a schooner instead of a cutter, and with no strake of their original planing left in their hulls.

There was the famour *Arrow*, for example, built at Lymington in about 1821, whose lines were taken from a French smuggler that had been wrecked on the Hampshire coast; for those were the days when the French knew more about how to shape a ship than ourselves. She was raced successfully, and then for some years lay neglected in a mud berth. It was more than a quarter of a century after her first appearance that she found a new owner who wholly replanked the yacht and apparently changed almost every characteristic of her form except that of the midship section. I believe it was of this sale that G. L. Watson spoke when he said of the purchase price that it had been cheap for a yacht but expensive for a midship section.

A few years later, after the visit of the *America*, she was again rebuilt, being increased by 17 ft in length with the addition of a long, hollow-lined bow. Now this was the end of her metamorphoses. In 1874 she was again lengthened, and almost sixty years after her first appearance she was racing successfully against the newest yachts of the day.

In that period when the barrel-bowed hull form of the eighteenth and early nineteenth centuries was being discarded and long lean bows were becoming fashionable, the major operation of increasing a yacht's length was lightly undertaken. There are scores of examples of its being performed on yachts simultaneously with other alterations of a less radical but often major character. The *Alarm*, starting life as a 193-ton cutter ended it, after almost total rebuilding when she had been found to be rotten, as a 248-ton schooner. The *Phantom*, a 20-tonner built at Poole in 1852, was rebuilt by Joseph White of Cowes as a 25-tonner.

In America as much as in England extensive alterations to existing yachts were made. As striking a career in this respect as any on either side of the Atlantic was that of the *Gracie*, which was launched in July 1868 and was, I believe, still sailing in the twentieth century. During the course of her career her length was increased from 60 ft 3 in. to 80 ft 0 in., her beam from 18 ft 8 in. to 22 ft

5. The Fastnet Rock

*Photo: Irish Press*

6. Yacht Marinas in Miami, Florida

*City of Miami News Bureau*

7. Corner of the huge Bahia Mar Marina at Fort Lauderdale

*Bahia Mar Publicity*

8. Cadet Week, Burnham on Crouch

*Trevor Davies*

5 in., her internal depth from 5 ft 6 in. (for she began her life as a typical shallow American centreboarder of the period) to 7 ft 0 in. and her draught from 5 ft 0 in. to 6 ft 8 in. Apart from these major alterations her ballasting was frequently modified, and finally she had all but 16 tons hung outside on the keel, whereas originally it had been wholly internal. One may wonder what of the original *Gracie* but the name remained in the final longer, broader, deeper vessel into which she was transformed.

## THE BEST BOAT FOR YOU

What is the best boat for you? The answer to this question usually seems clear to most people, who begin with a dream, until they have had the opportunity to materialize it. Then it is found to have been wrong. Again and again one sees people buying, or even having designed for them, boats that are not going to suit them because they have misjudged their own tastes, not clearly envisaged what they want the boat for, failed to analyse completely their personal boat-owning problem. Even experience does not always eliminate these errors of choice, for where yachts and boats are concerned, sea fever is always present to jog the judgement. When experience is lacking, the right answer will be struck only by the greatest luck.

People often buy a boat for quite irrelevant reasons – because they like the look of her, because she seems a snip, because she is a rugged seagoing vessel, because she is fast, because the wife likes the layout. No particular good qualities in a boat are germane to the issue of whether or not she is suitable until the purposes for which she is required have been clearly visualized.

And this is not often easily done, for the motives for wanting a boat are usually mixed and sometimes conflicting. Choosing the right boat is as much a psychological and philosophical matter as a technical one. Which is why one yacht architect has put high on the list of qualifications for the profession the power to read a client's mind better than he can read it himself.

To help subalterns, and much more senior officers as well, to collect their scattered thoughts, in my day the Army laid down a system of reasoning to be followed when facing an operational problem. I have lately tried the system on a couple of prospective owners who at first were fairly, though not completely, sure of the kind of boats that would suit them. In both cases their ideas were modified after applying what we may call the Military Method.

The process of reasoning is gone through under four headings: (i) Object; (ii) Factors; (iii) Courses open; (iv) Plan; and in that order. There is usually an immediate pause at heading (i), for as we have observed, the motives for boat owning are usually mixed. But something must be tentatively decided under this heading if a suitable choice is to be made.

The Factors heading comprises numerous matters with finances often the most important, but including many others such as time available for sailing, whom you want to sail with, family ties or help, the evergreen mooring problem. You make a list of every factor having some bearing upon ownership of a boat including not only those at present but also, so far as may be foreseen, in the future.

At this point you may find that the object begins to wobble, that it has been injudiciously chosen, and you may have to start again with a modified object. Once a concordat has been established between the object and the factors or has not, as the case may be, when you may decide to stick to fishing – the courses open may be considered, which in our connection will be chiefly concerned with the actual boats available that will fulfil the object, which you will already have established as both practicable and desirable.

This part of the process will probably resolve itself into a list of boats or types. The last step, the plan, will be the practical measures you will take to find, buy or build the boat.

I have known a man who, judging by his success, must have had a shrewd business head. He was in late middle age, liked his comforts, and had some but not considerable experience. He was a person I should describe as liking the accompaniments of yachting and the travel element rather than seagoing as an activity. The boat for him would have been a motor-sailer with the emphasis on power (preferably with twin engines), comfortable below deck, and with enough sail to suggest to the world that he was a salt at heart. Unfortunately, though intelligent, he was a little like a cushion and readily took the impress of the last person to sit on him. In a milieu of pretty hardened sailing people, in which he was not unimportant because he was a good organizer and the kind of person whose judgement on many matters was respected, he bought himself an offshore racer. He never intended to race to any serious extent, but presumably he felt the boat would give him an aura appropriate to his surroundings. Also she was a bargain, and his business instinct may have misled him.

I am convinced that had he reasoned through his ownership problem by the Military Method – and he was no fool – he would have obtained at first shot instead of second the yacht suited to him.

## ESTIMATION OF BUILDINGS COSTS

Accurate cost estimation is not easy, and in the larger shipyards it is the responsibility of a special department of trained people who do nothing else. On this department much depends, for slipshod quotation is able to lose contracts that might, even at a reduced figure, have been profitable.

It is sometimes found that a building contract from one yacht yard is double that from another, and large, if less striking, discrepancies are common. Though these may not necessarily mean that a mistake has been made, it is at least a possibility. I have in mind one case of an *under* estimate when a yard quoted, and ultimately had to accept, a figure some 20 per cent less than the economic value of a large job. Though the mistake was genuine enough – a clerical oversight – the client refused to make good the balance; and not surprisingly, for in accepting the yard's original figure he had rejected a number of only slightly higher quotations. We will consider some of the problems involved in quoting accurately.

The fair estimation of cost is so difficult that few of the smaller yards know accurately how much profit they make on a boat;

which is why, perhaps, they rarely claim to have made anything
but a loss – though this is a habit shared with many shipyards,
in spite of the profit on the annual balance sheet they cannot dis-
guise. For purposes of estimation, we may break down cost under
ten headings: (1) basic hull; (2) ballast; (3) internal joinerwork and
furnishing; (4) mast and spars; (5) rigging; (6) fittings, internal
and deck; (7) sails; (8) wages; (9) overheads; (10) profit. Wages,
though calculated initially under the separate headings, are totalled
in (8), so that the other items where they are not sub-contracts,
are for material only. Several headings may be mainly or
wholly, sub-contracted work – e.g. fittings, iron keel, sails. These,
of course, include the sub-contractors' wages in the purchase
price.

With accurate accounting, the basic hull and ballast will be
found to represent a surprisingly small proportion of the total
cost, though the sight of a fully planked and decked hull in the
shed may seem like a nearly completed yacht. The total under the
wages heading will, on the other hand, be a very large proportion
of the total, and any time-consuming work, which includes nearly
everything that suggests 'yacht finish', has a disproportionate effect
on the total cost. In the standard of finish demanded, an owner
therefore has an effective proportion of the price under his control.
But much that is included in the wages he cannot control.

If we consider two equally well-finished yachts of the same standards of construction, it will be seen that any wide variation in the
prices quoted by two yards can reasonably only be due to (a)
overheads; (b) profit; (c) bad organization reflected in the wages;
or (d) mistakes in estimating. Overheads are usually based on a
percentage of the estimated cost, excluding profit. It will be clear
that a client pays for bad organization in two ways: first, by an
increase under the wages heading due to time wasted, for if this is
habitual in the yard, it will become the standard on which they
base their wage estimates; and secondly by an increase in the overheads, which are inflated by the greater cost resulting from additional wages. Inevitably, the small, well-organized yard, in which
few people are engaged in other than productive work, should be
capable of producing a yacht with a high standard of finish at an

appreciably lower price than the large yard. The latter is also handicapped by more difficult problems of overseeing, and with time sheets that are likely to be in less close touch with reality. One advantage that they might have, of obtaining materials cheaper because in bulk, is lost today when they probably have few yachts on the stocks and no certain order book for the future.

The small yards, however, are not so likely to have evolved a rational system of estimating, and may lose a part of their advantage from this. There is also likely to be less method in the ordering of materials, with resulting delays which will appear under the wage heading. I should mention the danger of price estimation based on the Thames Measurement. If we consider the above method of breaking-down cost in terms of T. M., its absurdity is evident. It assumes that cost varies as the square of the beam; that the influence of beam, in fact, is vastly predominant over that of every other feature in determining price.

In fact, it has only a slight influence on (1), and no more rational influence on any of the others than the diameter of the steering wheel. The other items entail either the totalling of sub-contract prices, or the calculation of quantities and prices, all of which may be achieved with fairly close accuracy. The one item which is liable to an error that is not easy to predict is (8), the wages, which are affected by changes of rate, delays in obtaining material, weather and other imponderables.

Amongst the heaviest costs of the yard, apart from wages, are the materials involved in (1), the basic hull. The fact that this item bulks less predominantly in the final price analysis is due to the high price of labour, of fittings, and of detailed work below deck. Once information has been collected of the costs of various hulls, the most intelliegnt method of estimating the price under this heading is by means of a cubic number composed of the produce of the overall length, the beam, and the internal depth from the coachroof to the top of the wooden keel. For similar materials and standards of construction, prices are closely proportional to this numeral, and allowance may readily be made for fluctuations in the price of timber.

But the numeral must be used with discernment. I have seen a yard use this numeral in a way that operated strongly against the interests of the client. The design under consideration had a short bowsprit and bumpkin. It was proposed to draw out the profile of the stem and the counter to eliminate these – an increase in length of about 5 ft 6 in. – which dispensed with the spars and their attendant ironwork and staying. Probably the constructional work was cheapened, for the amount of additional planking was not great, and the work of two other trades, apart from ship-wrights, was rendered unnecessary. But, by putting the modified hull through a new cubic number calculation, the work was assumed to involve an increase in length of 5 ft 6 in. added in the middle of the ship, and a substantial addition to the cost appeared.

Costing is a subtle and time-consuming matter, in which shrewd judgement plays an important part. But it is likely that the time spent on it will repay yards by bringing contracts that they might otherwise lose. This does not mean the cutting of prices until the profits hang on a shoe string; but it does mean that there is consistency.

The economy that had once been expected from the line pro-duction of plastic hulls has not yet materialized, even it appears – at least for sizes up to about 8 tons displacement – in the USA, where the cost of shipwrights' work is appreciably higher than in Europe. The economy affected by building stock moulded hulls seems to be offset by the advertising expenses needed to sell the large production. Our small craft, it would seem, are following the commercial example brilliantly set by Coca-Cola. The ex-penditure on the product is a trifle compared with the cost of advertising it. Psychometrics, which is the science of selling things, I am told, has entered the boatyards, and the psyche-engineers may soon be more important than the shipwrights.

## THEY PREFER THEM EXPENSIVE

It has been said before that the expense of the modern yacht is in big measure due to the amount and elaboration of the equipment she carries on, above and below deck. It is surprising to find how relatively cheap a well-built hull with spars, rigging and adequate joinerwork may be if mechanical, electrical and other purely luxurious refinements are curtailed.

Yet there is another side to the question. Recently, visiting a small motor-sailer – the fifth of her type – I remarked to the builder on the lavish standard of her equipment. Lifelines were on chrome stanchions; there was a beautifully engineered self-stowing winch for hoisting a mainsail which could have been set up easily by a halyard with a single purchase; the water supply below was delivered by press-buttons; in the deckhouse were RDF and an echo sounder (but no chart table); and the furnishing below was truly gorgeous. I suggested that if a few score items, some of them quite small though in the aggregate costing a good deal, were eliminated, a handsome but moderately priced boat would result.

'That's all been worked out,' the builder replied. 'And the simpler edition could be reduced to two-thirds of this boat's price. But,' he added, 'we wouldn't be able to sell it. People prefer them like this and hang the cost.'

So there you are! Builders naturally like to sell an expensive rather than a cheap article. It is one of the most enjoyable ways of satisfying the customer. Nor is the owner's trend of taste to be deprecated so long as there is the money to satisfy it. A few independently-minded people may continue to believe that over-elaboration in small craft simply increases the worry without adding to real seaworthiness or even comfort afloat, if this quality is properly understood, and choose their craft accordingly. But let the rest indulge expensive and interesting tastes to the benefit of builders and equipment manufacturers and the great interest of the architects, who naturally prefer the sophisticated to the simple.

## THE RESPONSIBILITY OF LLOYDS

It appears from time to time that the precise implications of classification by Lloyd's are misunderstood by owners, and that the shortcomings of a yacht are visited upon the Society without justification. It is not impossible for a classed yacht with her surveys up to date to be radically unseaworthy. It is unlikely, but not impossible. And her unseaworthiness may not be an oversight of Lloyd's.

The society try in their rules to cover all the principal features of construction and equipment on which security depends. But the security of a ship, like the efficiency of a soldier, may ultimately rest on the last gaiter button, and no formulation of rules capable of administrative application can codify every detail. Primarily, Lloyd's rules are devoted to:

(1) The scantlings of the various members of the hull.
(2) The materials of which they are made.
(3) The methods by which they are held together.
(4) The adequacy of the equipment on which safety depends.
(5) The continued soundness in service of all the above.

The first four objects are achieved in the progress of the design and construction of a yacht. The fifth is assured so far as possible by the periodical surveys that are obligatory for a yacht that is to retain her class.

Lloyd's primary function is to assure adequate strength and good technique in the construction of the hull. In comparison with the detailed requirements of the rules in this connection, masting, sails and rigging are cursorily treated: 'All yachts are required to have their masts, spars, rigging . . . and sails in sufficient number and in good condition . . . in view of the difference in practice in regard to the masting and rigging of yachts these fittings are left to the judgement and experience of yacht owners, builders and designers.'

This, you may think, is rather easy-going; yet a little reflection will suggest that practicable, statutory masting and rigging re-quirements, apart from being difficult to reconcile with initiative in design and subsequent modifications, would do no more than scratch the surface of the problem. For excellence in sails, rigging and their fittings depends on constant watchfulness over details. We have to consider what is possible, and clearly a tabulation of rules and a routine of frequent, full surveys, which alone could assure a fixed standard in these matters, is not in this category. Owners would not submit to it, nor pay for it. They are not always models of agreeableness in what they do have to accept now; so many yachts lose their class.

It should be mentioned that for auxiliary yachts with less than 50 b.h.p. the classification does not depend on the engine or its installation, except in so far as these may effect seaworthiness through stern tube or sea connection fittings. Whether the engine goes, whether it causes acute vibration, whether it drives through a propeller that makes a hole in the water, are not the concern of Lloyd's. Nor do Lloyd's judge the merits of design: 'Responsibility for ensuring sufficient stability and proper trim does not rest with the Society.'

So it may be seen that a yacht classed up to date at the beginning of the season before last may be crank, floating deep, with an engine that rarely works, and a propeller that cannot drive the boat home over a mild, spring ebb. Changes may have been made in her rigging since the last survey, new fittings on deck may be neither strong enough nor properly fastened. Two seasons of neglect of the sails may have destroyed the strength that was enough to get them through their last survey. Perhaps the yacht has spent two seasons under a Mediterranean sun, with nobody bothering to wet her thin laid decks daily while her owner aired himself on a succession of bikini-covered beaches. And the accumulation of labels from the bottles of lager kept in the bilge may have compressed themselves tidily (knowing that there is not much room in a small boat) in the strum box of the bilge pump.

Such a yacht might make water with serious rapidity at sea. Inattention to laid decks during only one year have placed a yacht in danger of sinking when taken suddenly to sea. She might be filling rapidly, with sails blowing out, and no engine to hold herself off a lee shore. Yet there need have been no error in her survey report.

The situation has perhaps been laboured in the manner of an over-heated politician struggling to justify himself before the arrival of the first rotten egg. It would be bad luck if a classed yacht came to this pass in a short time. It may serve to emphasize, however, that Lloyd's produce a reasonable assurance of seaworthiness, but cannot guarantee it.

E

## CRUISERS – HEAVY AND LIGHT

I have noticed, and have commented elsewhere, upon a fact that I understand yacht brokers have also recognized; which is, that yachtsmen on the whole like moderately heavy displacement yachts. There are many yachtsmen who talk little about design, though their advice on the best sort of cabin table, the quickest way of hoisting a dinghy, or the most comfortable anchorage in Loctudy, is well worth the price of a round of drinks. They are also very quick at sizing up the fitness of a boat for their particular purpose, which also happens, if we exclude the – is it millions? – of dinghy sailors, to be that of a majority of yachtsmen. And they like fairly heavy boats.

This view may seem retrogressive, and with an air about it of the God of our fathers known (only too well, alas! it may be felt) of old. It may be dismissed as the ignorant braying of the lesser breeds without the light displacement law – without even the intelligence perhaps to understand it. Or it may be right. I believe that it is.

It is tedious to repeat that there are more yachtsmen afloat than ever before; but it is true. There are. What is more significant, however, is that people spend a higher proportion of their net income on yachts than ever before. I do not think that this can be attributed to the Englishman's love of sport, though I understand that it is celebrated throughout the world. It is not the result of a sort of Henry Newboltish 'Play up, play up, and play the game' enthusiasm translated, most expensively, from the cricket pitch to the Channel. A majority of the yachts above 5 tons are not primarily sporting instruments; they are the cottage in the country, the bungalow by the sea, which an owner has sacrificed in favour of a boat, and they are also the motor trip on the continent which the owner can no longer afford after paying the yard bills. They are an extension of life on shore, the home for that inconsiderable part of the week which England's weekend habit gives for leisure.

For these purposes small, light displacement boats are unsuitable.

This is not because they lack the necessary volume of space below the deck, for we know today how much room may be obtained inside light hulls. It is due to a natural law, which even a dizzy atomic age has not yet upset, and which makes it necessary for a floating body to displace a weight of water equal to its own weight.

Consider a cruiser of 8 tons T.M. Let her have scantlings equivalent in weight to the very reasonable requirements of Lloyd's Register, and a ballast ratio adequate for a sail plan which will drive her comfortably. Add an auxiliary engine of the power and reliability that the working yachtsman finds needful for his peace of mind. Provide a fuel tank to suit, and water tanks of enough capacity to save the owner, his wife, his children, and his friends from the horrors of the great unwashed. Make allowance for the fact that we are decadents at the tail end of a new Roman decline, and like electric light out of heavy batteries, food out of heavy tins or even heavier cold storage apparatus, and drink out of heavy bottles. Add the ever-increasing amount of gear which the owner, his wife, and his children collect, and his guests leave behind. Add the weight of water which the boat will absorb by soakage. Add the weight of the improvements which the owner never stops making. You will then find that you have either a 16-tonner or a fairly heavy displacement 8-tonner.

I have prints by me of a 16-ton cruising ketch on which the designer has pencilled with pleasing candour, the fully equipped load waterline. It lies four inches above the designed waterline and is produced by nearly 2 tons more weight. At her designed waterline the drawing shows a pretty heavy displacement yacht, but 2 tons more of displacement proved necessary even in this normal, comfortable cruiser. Yet attempts are made to produce cruisers of this size having less than three-quarters of her displacement; at least, such is shown on their drawings.

There is another aspect of the matter. The roughness of the ride which a boat will give to her crew is materially decreased by weight. In small boats the most trying motion is the one known technically as heaving, which is the bodily movement vertically of a boat through space. Weight reduces both the amount and the speed of these movements. The pitching period is a function of the displacement divided into the area of the load waterline, and from this relationship the effect of displacement upon comfort may be visualized.

There are yachtsmen interested purely in the sporting and competitive aspects of sailing. They will carry gin only because beer is too heavy, or nothing because the money saved on the gin will allow them to buy an American winch 5 per cent lighter and 500 per cent more expensive than the English article. These people are the salt of yachting progress. Designers love them, and rightly, being artists and technicians absorbed in problems which experiments help to solve. But most yachtsmen are comfortable, easy-going folk and prefer boats which are like themselves, and it is also to be noticed that the distinguished cruises which find their way into the Royal Cruising Club Journal, or which pick up the trophies of the Cruising Association, are usually undertaken in fairly heavy displacement boats. This may, as we have suggested, be simply the God of our fathers casting his long shadow. I shall believe that it is when somebody tells me how to make 10 tons of boat, gear and stores float with 8 tons displacement. If this cannot be done surely a boat designed initially for the heavier displacement is better than one pressed down to it in disregard of the drawings in which the form and proportions of the boat were settled with, one hopes, the highest refinements of careful judgement.

*        *        *

It is generally appreciated that displacement is weight, and that this weight represents the total quantities of various materials that cost money. Hence, within limits, light displacement means less cost, and for this sufficient reason has become popular today.

But since light displacement means smaller quantities of materials, it is worth considering how the reductions may be achieved, and which of the various components that combined make a yacht may most readily be reduced in amount.

For this purpose it is necessary to examine the composition of the total weight of the average yacht. The following figures have been produced from detailed weight calculations for three sailing yachts of normal cruising type and good modern design. The weight build-up may be averaged to the following percentages of the total displacement:

|  | per cent |
|---|---|
| Hull Structure | 30–43 |
| Ballast | 30–45 |
| Hull and deck fittings | 2–4 |
| Accommodation and furnishing | 3–7 |
| Mast, sails and rigging | 5–6 |
| Auxiliary and installation | 0–7 |
| Outfit (dinghy, cable, warps, etc.) | 2–4 |
| Load (fuel, water, stores, crew) | 6–8 |

Possibly the most striking feature of the above summary is the preponderance of the first two items – the hull structure and ballast. The former includes the whole of the constructional work from keel to deck canvas and coachroof, and also the paint. The latter consists of the ballast keel and such internal trimming ballast as may be carried. The two together make about 75 per cent of the total weight or displacement of the yacht.

Let us now consider the actual weights, based on this summary, of an average cruiser-racer of 30 ft on the waterline. For this length a displacement of 10 tons is the minimum for a normal type of hull, constructed to Lloyd's standards, with the internal space and amenities of a comfortable cruiser carrying a full outfit and a load of water, fuel, stores, and crew suitable for cruising. The allocation of the various weights would resemble that shown in Column A overleaf.

Let us now produce a light displacement cruiser-racer of the same waterline length, and to be modest in our requirements we will not aim at a displacement lighter than one of the old IYRU 8-Metres, many of which have been converted for cruising. We will take 8·2 tons as our target.

If the yacht is to be built to Lloyd's Rules we can expect no alteration in the constructional weights if, as may reasonably be

| | A<br>Moderate<br>tons | B<br>Light (i)<br>tons | C<br>Light (ii)<br>tons |
|---|---|---|---|
| Hull structure | 3·40 | 3.40 | 3·40 |
| Ballast | 4·00 | 3·25 | 3·25 |
| Hull and deck fittings | 0·30 | 0·30 | 0·25 |
| Accommodation and furnishing | 0·40 | 0·40 | 0·20 |
| Masts, sails and rigging | 0·50 | 0·40 | 0·40 |
| Auxiliary | 0·50 | 0·30 | 0·20 |
| Outfit | 0·20 | 0·20 | 0·20 |
| Load | 0·70 | 0·70 | 0·30 |
| | 10·00 | 8·95 | 8·20 |

so, the beam and draught of the lighter boat are the same as the heavier. This must therefore remain at 3·4 tons. We would like to retain a ballast ratio of about 40 per cent, as in the former boat, and on the lighter displacement of 8·2 tons will therefore be 3·25 tons. This is an appreciable saving, and for architectural reasons into which we need not delve – concerned with the relationship between displacement, stability, heeling moment, and resistance – this lesser amount of ballast would provide sufficient stability for an area of sail suitable for driving the lighter displacement hull. The rig, being smaller in area, may be lighter, and we may take a figure of 0·4 tons instead of 0·5 tons. But if now, having produced a light displacement hull with plenty of room in it, we proceed to follow natural instincts and put into it the same weights of furnishing, gear, water, and stores, we find that the displacement is not 8·2 tons but 8·95 tons; and this in spite of the fact that we have fitted a smaller auxiliary. (Light (i) shown in B above.)

We have still saved almost a ton in weight, but this particular boat is not satisfactory. Her sail area is too small for her displacement, her ballast ratio (36 per cent instead of the intended 40 per

cent) is not big enough to allow more sail area to be carried profitably. She would probably be slower than the heavier boat in all
weathers. It will be evident that to produce the light displacement
hull we are after it will be necessary to cut away considerably more
material from somewhere.

This has been done in Light (ii). The process has involved re-
ducing the weight of such hull and deck fittings as the sidelights,
stanchions, windlass, the fuel and water tanks, and the batteries.
The accommodation and furnishing has been halved in weight,
with all that this entails in terms of galley fittings, plumbing, cup-
boards, drawers and wardrobes, and other amenities below deck.
The fuel, water, and stores carried has been slashed by 57 per cent.
We now have, loaded and ready for sea, a real light displacement
cruiser-racer. She will be cheaper to construct than the Moderate
yacht, with three-quarters of a ton less metal in her keel, 4 cwt
less material and joinerwork below deck, less sail area, and lighter
gear.

We may, however, resent the relatively spartan accommodation,
and miss the water and stores that might have been carried. The
hull constructional weights might then be reduced by 0·4 ton by
adopting lighter methods of construction. Lloyd's might accept
this as a special submission, but the methods of construction that
would have to be adopted would require good workmanship
to combine the strength and lightness. The saving in cost of the
lighter keel would be swallowed in the higher price of the shipwrights' work, and the final price of this light displacement boat
would be much the same as the one of medium displacement.
But having saved 0·4 ton, the furnishing and accommodation of
the former might be of the standard of the latter.

It will be apparent that light displacement is a distinct economy
when it is obtained by reductions in the joinery work of the accommodation and furnishing, and by the simplification of the standard
of life to be led on board that is reflected in the lighter weight of
the load carried. It is logically most effective in small craft where
price is important and spartan conditions are naturally acceptable.
Whether light displacement can claim any positive advantage in
larger yachts, in which economy is less important than a standard

of comfort compatible with the yacht's dimensions, is more doubtful. Light displacement may be achieved, at a cost, in such yachts, and without sacrifice in accommodation; but it is not easy to put one's finger on the advantage of a yacht of 40 ft on the water-line and displacing 15 tons over one in the medium (not heavy) category of the same length and displacing 19–20 tons.

## THE FORTY PER CENT FICTION

The sky is blue and has been for some days. The sullen mud of the boatyards has hardened and those damp, dark sheds are being visited by exploring sunlight; sometimes by great beams of it as the doors are rolled back, which tried and failed to resist the winter draughts, and now let in the warmth and let out the boats. Already some of them are afloat, and as usual in spring, before the eye had become accustomed to their characteristic attitudes on the water, you notice those details of flotation that familiarity will soon cause you to pass over – here a boat clearly deeper than was ever intended when she was conceived on paper (and yet she has little gear on board yet and empty tanks), there, surprisingly, one down by the head even before the mast has been stepped; there, there, and there boats heavily down by the stern, yet each one of them waiting for a fat owner to take the helm.

Apart from taking out or re-stowing any inside ballast they may have, little can probably be done about old boats that are too deep or badly trimmed. But it is depressing when new yachts appear that are clearly floating deep initially, or just on their de-signed line without allowance made for soakage or accretions of gear. For those who spend much time each year studying designs of yachts building or just built, it becomes clear that the displace-ment and ballast figures quoted on them are often inconceivable, and that either the boat is going to float deep initially or the claimed ballast ratio is a fiction intended for good publicity.

It is a pity that with the modern cruiser-racer is has now become a point of professional pride to claim a 40 per cent-plus ballast ratio, for in most cases this is not and cannot be achieved in prac-tice. But the claim leads to all sorts of evasions and diplomatic falsehoods on drawings and sets of data, which in the end help nobody. We might call it the 40 per cent fiction. It is a principle irrationally reverenced.

We all know the designers' real difficulties in regard to ballast keel weights. What with inaccurate moulds, varying densities of keel metal, especially when lead is used, and faults in the casting they are faced here with one of the most anxious constructional problems. Errors are frequent, and often unavoidable by the designer, and he deserves sympathy. The most accurate and painstaking of them have had their lives embittered by controversies over keel weights, some of which threaten to lead to the law courts. We are concerned not with such undeserved misfortunes but with reasonable initial design and honest statements about what has been done.

The importance of adequate freeboard in the hard-sailed yachts of today has become well known. Freeboard is a basic design dimension to be settled at an early stage in blocking out the design, considering it in relation to the buoyancy in the overhangs and the displacement. There is a useful ratio, which deserves as much publicity as the ballast ratio – the reserve buoyancy/displacement ratio expressed as

$$\frac{\text{Volume of hull above the water}}{\text{Volume of hull below the water}}$$

The most important lesson learned from the modern habit of racing and cruising hard offshore has been that this ratio should be large. The *Myth of Malham* gave publicity to the fact, which has been generally recognized ever since, and was not wholly unrealized before. From the point of view of sea-keeping qualities a certain minimum is desirable, governed largely by the displacement and the character of the overhangs. It does seem common sense that this minimum should be achieved under average sailing conditions after a few years afloat. Then, unless displacements are heavier than those usually chosen today, the actual ballast ratio under sailing conditions is likely to be more like 35 per cent than 40 per cent.

For example, moderately full tanks, stores, crew and their gear will add about a ton to the weight of a yacht displacing 10 tons without these items, and she will never go to sea without these items unless she breaks adrift from her moorings. If her keel weighs 4 tons her ballast ratio will be 40 per cent on the moorings, but never more than 36 per cent at sea. I suggest she should have been designed initially for the bigger displacement and the smaller ballast ratio confesssed. Several factors, including her freeboards and the dispositions of her weights, might then have been advantageously modified.

Designers have to please their customers, and the unrealistic 40–45 per cent ratio has, through too much publicity, become accepted by many yachtsmen as normal for efficient design work; so architects have to strain for it, at least on the drawings, and in the process distort the facts of the situation. I think it likely that when soakage and additions to the ship's gear over the years are taken into account as well as stores and kit, many of the first-class cruiser-racers of today are performing well with ballast ratios of less than 35 per cent. What is needed is the climate of opinion in which designers may produce drawings that are in accordance with the facts of life.

After all structural weights, other weights and the related ratio of ballast to displacement are the most vital criteria of performance under sail. If, when dealing with such matters, we get into the habit of living in a fairy-tale land and distorting basic facts and figures, a great deal of nonsense is liable to follow. Indeed, it seems to me that it already *has* followed.

Yet we may sometimes not be in fairyland even when ballast ratios exceeding 50 per cent are claimed; but we may be sure then that we are concerned with an unusual, specialized craft of expensively sophisticated construction.

Peter Nicholson has told me that the actual measured ballast ratio of the successful offshore racer *Quiver IV* was 52 per cent *with all gear aboard* and after the yacht had been afloat for about three weeks. But *Quiver IV* was a heavy displacement yacht with light displacement construction, having double skin Honduras mahogany planking all glued and laid on fairly closely spaced mahogany frames. Weight saving was as conscientiously practised in all departments as it is in extremely light displacement craft; and when this is done in one of moderately heavy displacement an arresting ballast ratio may be achieved. But Peter Nicholson agrees that 52 per cent represents about the limit possible for wooden yachts able to withstand being driven hard offshore.

★     ★     ★

Ballast ratios have always been with us, and much higher than those we know today. There is no virtue in *mere* bigness of ballast ratio; it may be obtained simply by adding to the weight of the keel. You may go on doing this until the yachts sinks, and immediately beforehand achieve a ballast ratio in excess of 90 per cent. At a more rational level the defunct IYRU 6-Metre class boats had ballast ratios of 60 per cent; and 66 and more per cent ratios were found in the plank-on-edge cutters of the '80s – the extreme cruiser-racers of their period. In modern times ballast ratios have come into prominence only since the war, their use being encouraged by the general trend towards lighter displacements.

It is as easy to design some sort of light displacement yacht as it is to design one with a big ballast ratio by simply adding weight to the keel. To produce the lightweight version you take weight off the keel. But the only way to produce a good light displacement boat is to assure that, though light, she retains much the same proportion of her total weight in the keel as the heavier boat.

Let us set this proportion at 40 per cent for average light or heavy displacement good designs to deep draught and moderate beam. If then we design a boat having *Quiver IV*'s waterline length of 35 ft and the generous displacement of about 14 tons, we should aim at a keel of 5·6 tons, leaving 8·4 tons for all the other weights. If, however, we aim at a light boat of this length, displacing only 10 tons, we shall need a keel of 4·0 tons – 1·6 tons less than that of the heavier yacht – but there will still be only 6·0 tons instead of 8·4 tons for the remaining weights. The difference of 2·4 tons of weight will have to be saved by means of lighter

construction, which must still be strong enough, lighter joinerwork, simplicity below deck (there will of course be less space in
which to become complicated in the lighter yacht) and careful
weight saving in every item. All this demands skill, expense often,
and sacrifice of comfort.

But it is the only way of producing a fast, light displacement
seagoing yacht. The ballast ratio is the crucial index of its potential
ability. There is another way of producing a light displacement
yacht; it is drawn as such and with a little more than enough freeboard; the keel turns out to be a little lighter than expected, but
what with one thing and another and all the drawings flashing
about, this is overlooked; the waterline creeps a few inches up-
wards while being cut-in; a beautiful boat-topping confuses the
issue. The end is a boat of moderate displacement, small ballast
ratio, and deficient freeboard. She will be tender and slow. Hence
it is that in our own day, when yachts of light and medium-light
displacement have become common, there is an anxiety to qualify
for that only Order of Merit, a *sufficient ballast ratio.*

It is otherwise with the heavier displacement yachts which,
when produced by reputable designers and builders, are able to
achieve an adequate ballast ratio without any anxious weight
saving. A notably heavy displacement cruising ketch by James
McGruer in 1950 had a ballast ratio of 44 per cent, though neither
in construction nor joinerwork and appointments below deck
was she other than substantial. This is the reward of heavy displacement.

What Camper & Nicholsons have done is to design yachts of
what today may be regarded as fairly heavy displacement, and
then devote to their construction and fitting-out the sense of
dedication to weight saving that has formerly been reserved for
light displacement yachts. The result is a ballast ratio of 52 per
cent, which in the circumstances is more readily believable than
the claimed 40 per cent of many other yachts.

As a general study in ballast ratios, the table may be considered.
The relevant data for *Quiver IV* appear in the first column; those
for a lighter displacement yacht in the second, both yachts being
of the same waterline length:

|  | Quiver IV | Light Displacement Example |
|---|---|---|
| Waterline length | 35·0 ft | 35·0 ft |
| Displacement | 14·43 tons | 11·0 tons |
| Ballast | 7·59 tons | 4·4 tons |
| Ballast/displacement ratio | 52% | 40% |
| Weight available otherwise | 6.84 tons | 6·60 tons |

The light displacement example, of 11·0 tons, is not as extreme as some successful yachts, such as the Giles-designed *Miranda III*, which initially displaced this amount on a waterline 4 ft longer.

It may be seen from the table that if the light displacement yacht has a ballast ratio of 40 per cent, the weight available for everything else will be 6·6 tons. But *Quiver IV*, with a 52 per cent ballast ratio, has 6·84 tons, or a quarter of a ton more available. *Quiver IV*'s construction need not be much heavier than that of the lighter boat. If both boats were built to Lloyd's rules and had (as they might) the same length and draught measurements, their scantling numerals would vary with the beams, which might differ little. With a quarter of a ton of spare weight to play with, it will be evident that no miracle of construction is needed to assure *Quiver IV*'s weight of ballast.

When measured for the displacement figure shown in the table, the yacht was fully equipped, including food, 15 gallons of fuel, 33 gallons of water and a certain amount of personal gear. All sails were stowed and the dinghy and life-raft were on board. Yet need we be so surprised about that 52 per cent ballast ratio?

These detailed considerations of ballast ratio lead naturally to the more general question of the relative merits of the fairly heavy and fairly light types of yacht. Whereas once the latter type tended to be associated with sophistication in design and the former with a certain homeliness, now both may be equally advanced in all respects. Then, purely from the point of view of performance, there really seems little to choose between them. Each has its merits and defects.

As Jack Laurent Giles said some years ago in a lecture: 'We have

seen in direct competition light and heavy displacements and . . .
(each) has gained prizes at one time or another. From time to time
a particular boat establishes a high reputation and wins a lot of
flags, only in later years to lapse into the general ruck. More often
than not we find that these outstanding boats belong successively
to particular owners, and we are forced to conclude that it is the
man rather than the boat that matters. That, however, is not to
deny that there are good and bad boats, but one cannot avoid the
impression *that the type of boat is unimportant.*' (My italics.)

In the small sizes a light displacement boat of the utmost simplicity below deck will provide the best offshore racing machine
at the lowest price. In the larger sizes, and above all when the best
and most advanced of either type is required without regard to
expense, the choice between them is not easily made, even when an
owner's requirements are clear-cut. If racing is the primary object,
the bias of the rating rule may be a determining factor; but as it
happens the RORC rule is remarkably successful in favouring
neither type.

When sailing to windward in smoothish water and enough
wind, speed is independent of displacement, neither light nor
heavy boat gaining any advantage from her type alone. When the
seaway gets up, the light boat still appears to suffer no disadvantage
apart from giving her crew a rougher ride, and this may be com-
pensated by the fact that with her smaller sail area her gear is
lighter to handle.

Under drifting conditions, the light boat's small sail area in
relation to wetted surface handicaps her; she is liable, as someone
once described it, to 'stick' to the water. But under fast reaching
conditions the merits are reversed. The slighter wave making and
easy run of the lighter boat enables her to hold bigger speeds in
quartering seas. This, in fact, is the least favourable point of sailing
for *Quiver IV* and her type.

It is perhaps harder to maintain a light displacement boat at its
most highly tuned. Its sensitivity to weight and weight adjustments makes it a sensitive instrument. And it is also probably
harder to steer well. The need is for a lighter hand and the type
is less forgiving of momentarily slack reactions than heavier

sisters. But there are conditions when the latter may be the harder to control. When racing and close reaching in heavy conditions, their greater weight and usually longer lateral plane may make their control a trial of strength no less exacting than the trial of quickness presented by the lighter yacht.

## *VEE-ON-ROOT-L*

Not infrequently we speak of the speed-length ratio, or $\sqrt{\dfrac{V}{L}}$, which is

$$\frac{\text{speed in knots}}{\sqrt{\text{waterline length in feet}}}$$

Its reiterated use may justify a note on its origin, and an explanation of why it is a convenient, indeed an essential, basis for many comparisons between ships or yachts.

The speed-length ratio is not a piece of dignified obscurity used by naval architects to hide emptiness of their minds, but the only means of making certain comparisons valid. There was a time when, for lack of knowledge of its function, Leonardo da Vinci came to several erroneous conclusions whilst studying the resistance of bodies in water, and four centuries later Vice-Admiral Frederik Chapman was similarly misled. When dealing with the speeds of aeroplanes, railway trains, satellites, or even fully submerged submarines, the speed-length ratio is unnecessary, for no aspects of their design are affected by it. But a ship proceeds on the surface of a fluid medium, the sea, producing for this reason waves when in motion, and her manner of wave creation is directly influenced by her length.

It was the study of wave formations created by ships and models that first led to an understanding of the speed-length ratio. Observations revealed that at certain speeds the wave pattern thrown by a model exactly resembled, so far as it could be measured, that produced by the ship. The small wave formation was a scale model of the large. It was found that this occurred when the speeds of the two hulls were in proportion to the square roots of their linear sizes. That is, if a 4-ft model were run at 2 knots, the pattern of its waves, its trim and behaviour in the waves were exactly the same as those of the 64-ft ship it might represent when making 8 knots, whilst an enlargement of the 64-ft vessel 100 ft long would also show a similar wave system when doing 10 knots. And the same would apply to all other speeds so long as they were in proportion to the square roots of the lengths involved.

This led to the discovery of further important facts. Let us consider a boat of 16 ft on the waterline and a one-quarter size model of 4 ft. When the boat is doing 4 knots her speed-length ratio

$\dfrac{V}{\sqrt{L}} = \dfrac{4}{\sqrt{16}} = 1$, and she will move with her waves in attendance,

drawing them along with her, the faithful mirror of her speed. And we have seen above that the 4-ft model of the boat at 2 knots will have an exactly similar retinue on a smaller scale, for at this speed her speed-length ratio will also be equal to unity. The other important fact is that when the boat and model are moving at the same speed-length ratio – at corresponding speeds as they are called – not only will their wave systems be similar, but their resistance due to wave-making will be *exactly the same per ton of displacement*. Divide the wave making resistance of the ship and model by their respective displacements and the same answer will be obtained in either case.

These facts are due to certain properties of gravity waves in water. Their speed is governed by their length from crest to crest, and is proportional to the square root of this length. Why should it be exactly the square root? Why indeed? Such waves are assumed to be of a trochoidal nature, which mathematically may be proved to have this period. Time and again in the analysis of natural phenomena we find a strange obedience to neat mathematics. Newton was able to explain the courses of the stars by a few simple rules, one of which was that every particle of matter in the universe attracts every other by a force proportional to the product of their masses and inversely proportional to the distance between them.

Why should this be? Somebody once suggested it was

because God was a mathematician. Such are what the unphilo-
sophical call 'laws of nature'; and we might more accurately say
that they are observed facts about nature caught in the web of
that variety of reasoning man has devised and called mathematics.
Hence, we say that the speed of a sea wave is proportional to the
square root of its length. If we express the matter in knots and
feet, we may say the speed is equal to $1.34 \sqrt{L}$.

If we turn from considerations of speed to those of energy, we
find that the energy contained in a wave system is proportional to
its length and to the square of its height. A full-bodied, heavy-
displacement yacht sets up a deeper wave system than one of light
displacement. The above fact about the energy in a wave system
explains why she is intrinsically slower and takes more driving.

The speed-length ratio is a criterion of the conditions under
which a boat is moving. Once the speed indicated by $V / \sqrt{L} =$
$1.34$ has been reached, something of importance has happened,
regardless of the size or type of ship. The wave system created by
the speed is then as long as the ship itself. Such may occur on a
broad reach in a stiff wind. There is a mounting crest under the
stem and counter; the stern wave may actually be lapping over
the archboard; and amidships, in the hollow trough of the wave,
the garboard may be seen. Photographers and artists like the condition of $V / \sqrt{L} = 1.34$. And under sail it represents nearly the
maximum speed attainable. For once the wave system due to
speed becomes longer than the ship creating it, the sea does something analogous to putting the brakes on. Higher speeds are possible, but difficult to achieve under sail, and cannot be held for
long.

Thus, whatever the size of a yacht, her wave throw and resistance are governed by the value of $V / \sqrt{L}$. At $V / \sqrt{L} = 1.34$
she rides on two wave crests, whilst at any higher speed she will
leave the stern crest abaft the hull. At $V / \sqrt{L} = 1.5$, a speed often
claimed but rarely achieved under sail, the wave system created
is 25 per cent longer than the hull, and the resistance it causes becomes very high indeed *in proportion to the displacement of the hull*.
It is this proportion that is important. It is governed by the speed-

F

length ratio, and comparisons between yachts, where it concerns hull form and resistance, are valid only at equal speed-length ratios, whilst maximum attainable speeds are governed wholly by it.

## SPEED UNDER SAIL

Speed is a quality that is unfailingly attractive in ships. Possessed of it, the ugly are forgiven. The unseaworthy have their most graceless faults overlooked, or are encouraged to wear them proudly, by admirers who are as blinded as those deep in the gay self-deceptions of love. Possessed of enough speed, a reputation is assured that will keep a ship's name sweet when others just as worthy have joined the millions of the unremembered. Who today can think of the name of a single East Indiaman off hand? But has anyone forgotten *Ariel*, *Thermopylae*, *Lightning*? Who recalls that an *Aquitania* was contemporary with the first *Mauritania*; yet there was only the little matter of a knot or so between the two?

Add to the glamorizing effect of speed the fact that under certain conditions, including the present age of yachting, it is an economic asset. Then remember that actual speeds through the water were never accurately assessed during the great days of sail, as indeed they rarely are now, and set this together with the psychological fact that the senses with which man judges speed are notoriously unreliable, and it will be seen that all the circumstances likely to upset sound judgement are present. And so more mendacious claims have been made, and still are being made, about speeds than about anything else in connection with ships.

How often do we find reports, particularly – if I may say so – from the USA, in which designers claim speeds of their fast motor boats which would not be reached if double the specified power were installed, and the boat hurled over the measured mile at full throttle with all the crew straining forward and holding their breaths and hats? Claims made in the present age of mechanical propulsion and accurate speed trials, by peolple who presumably expect to be believed, suggest how many of the high speeds claimed in the past and under sail may be without foundation.

It is a subject that has been examined in detail by the late Capt.

James Learmount, who was at one time master of the iron clipper *Brenhilda*. The first point he makes is that, by the time people became interested in accurate records of speed, the larger sailing ships had passed into history and first-hand evidence was difficult to find. Nor might such evidence be worth much when found. 'It is not generally recognized,' he writes, 'that the "record runs" claimed by various sailing-vessels in the ninetenth century *were never checked.*' (The italics are mine.) He compares such conditions with those found in modern yachting, and is possibly too favourable to the latter when he speaks of claimed speeds 'where every detail is verified by qualified observers'. With the exception of recent measured mile trials under sail, no assured measured speed records under sail in yachts exist, other than average speeds on passage.

Capt. Learmount takes a number of days' runs recorded in *Lloyd's Calendar*, and proceeds most convincingly to demolish their claims. They all involve day's runs exceeding 400 miles, and the ships are the famous American clippers by Donald Mackay which were built on spec. for the British market. Learmount points out first that the conditions under which the ships were built and sold inevitably encouraged excessive claims of speed. Secondly, the method of measuring speed through the water, with a Yankee log and a sand glass,[1] used under the formidable conditions of wind and sea inevitable at times of hard sailing, was amenable to the grossest error, which the author estimates even so high as 5 knots in some cases. Hence claims of 17 knots when the actual speed was 12 knots.

'In my experience,' writes Learmount, 'it has taken three apprentices, the officer of the watch and myself to haul in the line at that speed (12 knots). In the conditions that would prevail in a ship going at a much high speed, it is doubtful whether the master could have spared hands to be used for such an inessential job.'

'This recording of the hand log . . . was just an elaborate scheme of window dressing, expected by advanced agents . . . who did not miss an opportunity of getting full publicity for box-office purposes.' And Capt. Learmount proceeds to show how the speeds obtained from heaving the log cannot always be reconciled with the navigational record of the chart and the fixed positions. He considers one example, and we may wonder how representative it may be of many. Capt. Learmount's final conclusion is: 'From every angle, taking my long experience in sail into account, I do not believe any ship ever exceeded or even reached 400 miles in 24 hours under sail. I believe that the best day's run (noon to noon) ever to have been made under sail was that of the five-masted barque *Preussen*, when she made 370 miles under Capt. Peterson in the South Pacific. This, it may be noted, is a speed of a little less than 15½ knots.

When we examine some of the records claimed we find that, even were they acceptable, they are not high compared with modern offshore yachts. There were, for example, the two 24-hour runs of respectively 436 and 430 miles claimed by Donald Mackay's *Lightning* when under British ownership. The speed was thus 18·2 knots, and with her length of 244 ft the speed-length ratio was only 1·17.

Then there was the enormous *Great Republic*, of a size beyond the safe limit of length for a wooden ship that was to be hard driven, and built in a last vain endeavour to prove, in the face of the new iron-built ships, that America's great resources of timber still offered the best material for the shipbuilder. Her outstanding days' run of 413 miles represents a speed-length ratio of only 0·94, for her length was 330 ft. If we reduce the length of the day's runs to the more acceptable figures suggested by Capt. Learmount, we find that both the *Lightning*'s and the *Great Republic*'s speeds give speed ratios of less than 1·0, and the latter less than 0·85.

When we consider the stresses involved, and the tremendous powers needed even for this category of speed in heavy ships (about 3,000 h.p.), the higher claims are seen to be excessive. Yet we know that yachts achieve more, though certainly nothing like what often appears in records. This is to be expected, for with reduction in size the relationship between power needed and the strengths of materials becomes more favourable. And also the lesser powers required with the smaller ships allow the necessary amounts to be achieved in lower winds and slighter seaways. We may still, however, dismiss *Satanita*'s 17 knots claimed when sailing on a broad reach, and giving a speed-length ratio 1·75. Major Hunloke used to consider that 14 knots was the maximum speed of the smaller *Britannia*, and this was not an under-estimate. Indeed, I consider it probably an over-estimate. The most realistic of her high reputed speeds would seem to be the average she maintained of 12½ knots on the last lap on a Channel race in 1896. Here the speed-length ratio was a little more than 1·3 and most creditable at that.

It is worth remembering in connection with speeds at sea that they be checked by facts derived from physical laws, and these can quickly prove the nonsense of the more cheery and expansive assertions made by people with a mug in their hand and an elbow in the beer slop. On the basis of these, I think the following table is a pretty close estimation of maximum speeds through the water obtainable under sail by a modern yacht:

| Length waterline in ft | | 25 | 30 | 35 | 40 | 45 | 50 |
|---|---|---|---|---|---|---|---|
| V Speed in knots | | 7 | 7·7 | 8·3 | 8·9 | 9·4 | 10 |

I should add that such error that there may be is on the side of generosity. Only ideal conditions of wind and sea will allow the speeds shown to be achieved, and they will not occur offshore in an average seaway.

Before counter-claims are produced, the following facts should be remembered. We have seen that a speed-length ratio of 1·0 is about all that the clippers achieve at their fastest. To raise the ratio from 1·0 to 1·2 in any ships regardless of size entails the application of appreciably *more than double the power*. To raise the speed to a ratio of 1·3 will need a further doubling of the power. At a speed-length ratio of 1·4 the power requirement will be about seven times that at 1·0.

Consider for a moment the implication of such figures in one tangible example, a modern 35 ft waterline cruiser-racer. The yacht will need seven times more power at 8¼ knots than she does at 6 knots. It means a difference in wind strength between that at the middle of Force 4 and the top of Force 7.

And now consider what is entailed by yet one more of these knots so airily flipped about, and it will be seen that false claims quickly show their real colour.

## SAILING CLOSE TO THE WIND

When is the boat being pinched? When is she being allowed to wander off too much? When, in fact, is she being sailed so that she may get to that point up to weather in the quickest time?

We may become elementary for a moment and point out that the answer revolves round two issues:
(i) The distance to be sailed; (ii) The speed through the water. The interaction of the two produces the complications involved in this matter.

The first of the factors is a matter of simple calculation. In smooth water an inshore racer may point as close as 40 degrees to the true wind. In sailing from A to point B up to weather and at a distance of 100 cables (or miles or yards as you prefer) she must sail a distance of about 130 cables.

An unweatherly, full-bodied cruiser with a season's growth of weed on her bottom and an inefficient gaff rig may not point closer than 55 degrees. She will have to sail a distance of 174 cables, or nearly one-quarter as far again as the racer.

This is an impressive increase in distance, and the fact that these figures are representative respectively of smart and of undistinguished performers accounts partly for the spread out of the boats at the end of the windward leg of a handicap passage race with a menagerie fleet. We may round up the figures and say that for every degree farther off the wind that a boat is sailed, the distance that must be worked to windward (i.e. the distance sailed in proportion to the direct course) is increased by 2½ per cent.

Here we come upon the second factor, the speed. It may be seen that the cruiser in the example, if she is to reach the weather point at the same time as the racer when the latter is going through the water at 5 knots, will have to make a speed of 6½ knots. Every boat, as she is eased off the wind increases her speed up to a point, lying beyond our immediate interest, when the wind comes a little abaft the beam. The problem that has to be determined is whether the speed gained is enough to compensate for the considerably greater distance that must be sailed to reach the weather point.

The general answer – we are concerned here with generalities only – is that the degree of closeness to the wind that may profitably be sailed is a direct function of the efficiency of hull and rig in their respective capacities of hydrofoil and aerofoil. The efficient combination is able to maintain a high speed whilst sailing close to the wind. The most effective combination loses some of its efficiency in broken water, which has the effect of lowering the lift-drag ratio of the hull-keel combination, and must then be sailed less fine. The inefficient combination loses so much speed as a result of leeway angle (which, beyond a certain point, may become excessive leeway *drift* and further augment the distance that has to be sailed) that she must be sailed freer.

The following are speed figures derived from a boat sailing in a force 3 wind:

| Course to True Wind (degrees) | Speed (knots) |
|---|---|
| 45 | 4·2 |
| 55 | 4·5 |
| 65 | 4·6 |

It may be seen that at these speeds a better time to windward will be achieved at 45 degrees from the true wind than at 55 degrees. It is possible that in a seaway the speed at 45 degrees would drop in comparison with that at 55 degrees to an extent that might make the latter the more profitable course. And were speed figures available for angles between 45 degrees and 50 degrees it might be found that one of them would provide the shortest time to windward.

It would apparently be an ideal for the speed to windward in relation to the course sailed to be measured by sailing trials in a variety of wind strengths; then the best course to sail would be directly calculable, and might be presented in tabular form in terms of winds strength and angle to the wind. Unfortunately

the variables involved would probably make these data less trust-
worthy than the sense of a good helmsman. A change of sail or
sheeting would upset the data; and even if it could be ensured
that a boat always sailed with an identical trim in a given wind
strength, the same wind does not always knock up the same sort
of sea.

In the light of experience, at what points off the wind have
boats of various types proved to have their best speeds to windward? The following figures are offered as reasonably close estimates:

| Type | Angle of course to true wind (degrees) |
|---|---|
| Very smart inshore racers in smooth water | 38–43 |
| Cruiser-racer | 45 |
| Full-bodied cruiser, limited draught and Bermudian rig | 50 |
| Gaff cutter, smack form | 55 |
| Clipper ship | 65 |
| Ship of the line | 70 |

I regard the lowest figure for the inshore racer as distinctly
optimistic, but attainable perhaps during fleeting moments of
perfect sailing. When going about in a smart racing yacht it is
more usual to find that a mark must bear almost square off the
beam if it is to be laid with certainty. The figure for the cruiser-
racer applies to smooth water conditions. Going about offshore
a really smart boat usually seems to need about 100 degrees between tacks, so when there is a small slop in the sea the steady
course to windward is about 50 degrees off the true wind.

I have had a report of a cruiser of full body type but excellent
sails (a Gauntlet) making steady tacks through 80 degrees; but
this is surprisingly good. A friend of mine working up-Channel
this year against a north-westerly in a Falmouth Quay punt, which
had a badly-designed gaff rig as well as the inherent disadvantages
of her hull shape, found that the best the boat would do was to
tack through 130 degrees.

So he motored.

In a recent issue of *The Mariner's Mirror*, Sir Alan Moore is reported to have said: 'It is said that the larger decked boats can sail at two points from the wind.'

How many of us when racing, or returning to home shores, or getting away from them, have longed to believe that we were indeed within two points of the inevitable head winds of European waters.

Lt.-Col. H. G. Haslar took up Sir Alan Moore's remark in *The Mariner's Mirror*. He wrote:

'In the course of development work on small sailing yachts, I have made a particular study of the question of close-pointing, and have discussed it with various leading yacht-racing helmsmen. In my opinion, the facts are as follows:

'(1) Taking the expression "close hauled" to mean the point of sailing on which a boat makes its best progress to windward in smooth water, then there is very little variation (say, not more than two or three degrees) between the close-hauled courses of the best modern racing classes, *regardless of size.* . . .

'(2) The best yachts will not point effectively much closer than four points to the true wind – *certainly not as close as* 3½ *points.*'

The italics are mine.

# 4

# HELMSMANSHIP

## SOME HELMSMEN AND PRINCIPLES

I was talking the other day to a friend, whom I regard as the best all-round helmsman I know, about helmsmanship. The talk was decidedly personalized and partly unprintable. Later I settled down in the cockpit, as the sun went down and the heat drained from the last of the day, to make some notes on what we had said. Here first are a few of the more personal comments; some of them apply to helmsmen of an older generation I never knew, but not the majority.

*Helmsman A:* An actor, a Sir Henry Irving of the wheel. Brilliant on every point of sailing so long as there were enough pretty eyes on him throughout the race. But if the pretty eyes went below out of the rain and wind he might have been guiding a farm cart round the course. On the rougher days we used to have lined up ashore in the morning a collection of pretty girls who we knew could stick it for the duration in the cockpit, even though a little rough and wet. He owed his success in bad weather to their smiles and streaming curls.

*Helmsman B:* Excellent at the start or a crowded mark. Knew the rules inside out and unmerciful to anyone who didn't. There was no sentimental sportsmanship about him. He would seem to have been happy to carve a ship in half if she became wrongly placed and in his way – so everyone was terrified of him. Though the most amiable man ashore (but not it seems in his business capacity) at the start of a race or rounding a mark every other helmsman became his personal enemy. He invariably beat them – quicker and with more nerve – but a worse helmsman to windward you would have to go far over the seas to find. The helm was to him something to move, preferably with great violence, and if possible to the acute discomfiture of a neighbouring boat. For him sailing lost its glitter when there was sea room and just the wind to play with. Then he would stamp about on deck changing sails the whole time.

*Helmsman C:* No real good except to windward, and then outstanding. He was a designer as it happens. You cannot judge a helmsman's ability to windward until you have watched his performance in a one-design or closely restricted class on a windward leg when tide is unimportant. You must divorce his performance from tactics, a navigational sense, or local knowledge. He is engaged simply in making the best speed possible to windward for the boat. He is solving, instant by instant, instinctively, equations that our tank-testing experts present as daunting graphs. Or, to express it more humanly, he is like the rider as his horse rises to the fence and he says in his heart: 'We've got to stick closely together in this or make a muck of it.' The sticking together is not a matter of hanging on but of communion. It is the same with man and boats (to windward), man and horses, man and cars (when racing); a tingle in the wrists, a sensitivity to movement as some people have to poetry or music.

*Helmsman D:* A good all-round helmsman. He would rush into the melée of a crowded start with dark spectacles on and an expression of acute sadness. Sheets, sails, any lines lying about the deck seemed a thousand miles from his thoughts. The most he would ever say to anyone at this time might be a weak request to 'de-mist his specs'. Then, having thrown the boat about perhaps four times in a minute, gybed and re-gybed and hit the line on the gun, preceded only by seconds by a soft order relayed louder to the foredeck to hoist the spinnaker, he would glance at the shambles around on deck and say gently; 'We must clear up, mustn't we?'

He was a bad deck-hand and would never do such work himself, but he was not fragile. In Force 6–7 winds offshore with the biggest spinnaker unwisely set and a badly yawing boat, and gallons of water pouring over him regularly, though he would have discarded his dark specs, spiritually they were still on his nose. He might be having to work on the wheel or tiller violently, but it was done with the sure rhythm of an Andalusian housewife drawing water from the well. There was such a complete lack

of fuss that you felt anyone could be left with the helm. You discovered later the mistakes when the relief helmsman took
over.

What can we make from the above personal notes? I think there
are three distinct phases of helmsmanship each requiring quite
different qualities:

   (i) At the start and rounding crowded marks.

   (ii) Sailing to windward in clear water.

   (iii) Steering in free winds.

Helmsmanship as an art hardly enters into (i) at all. The qualities
required are quick judgement and the ability to size up a quickly
moving situation in a trice. It is the instinct of the good platoon
officer in battle, an innate sense of tactics. The important person concerned need not be holding the helm, though he invariably is
nowadays. He need only give quick orders.

Windward helmsmanship is the reverse of this state of affairs.
I have a theory that extroverts handle a yacht best at a start or
rounding marks, introverts going to windward and sometimes
when going downwind. We talk a lot about concentrating on the
helm and not distracting the helmsman. We see the truth of this
sometimes in ocean racing when, at the changes of watches in one
ship, another with different watch times suddenly begins to draw
ahead, though sailing level until this moment. But in fact sailing
a boat to windward is not so much a matter of concentration as
living in an ivory tower, out of which you may peer from time
to time to suggest the hardening or starting of this or another
sheet, but not to gossip in the cockpit. Sailing a boat well to windward is a matter of rhythm rather than consciously close attention.
It is almost a dreamy activity and the earnest man of action is
sometimes too fidgety to succeed. It is not an easy art to learn,
this remaining continuously in the rhythm of the boat. Indeed,
for the greatest performances it cannot be learned; but even the
most talented need constant practice. The rhythm that is being
followed is a constantly changing one with the everlasting slight
shifts of wind and the ever-varying character of the seaway – it is
not the beat of a metronome but the rising and falling measures of
plain song. No helmsman is all the time right in step with his boat,

but the best is quickly aware when touch is being lost and feels his way back.

The windward helmsman should not be asked to do anything else. He should not have to discuss tactics. If he is sitting down to leeward and with little view he should be quite unworried as to whether he is going to hit anything. He is drawing into a harmony wind, sails and sea; it is preoccupation enough.

Once off the wind in light weather and steering by compass or on a mark, the helmsman requires little skill beyond that minimum needed to hold a boat on a straight course. There are people who never learn to do this, but they are in a minority; though some take a long time to grasp the actions of a tiller, and it is common for beginners to swing it the wrong way in an emergency. In moderate weather the experienced helmsman when steering off the wind may reasonably be in control on deck and in charge of the sail trimming – with the help of a man up forward. The sails, which were his masters when sailing to windward are now his servants. Working to windward he pointed where the sails told him to go. Sailing freer he goes where he wishes and ensures that the sails are right for enabling him to do so as quickly as possible.

In higher winds on a reach and close reach the helmsman has to pay more attention to his helm and course. Some boats are hard – in the purely muscular sense – to steer on these points, and a boat of no more than 10 tons T.M. may be beyond the power of even an experienced woman. The most important operations involved lie in checking the often wild lunges up to windward and returning the boat to her correct pointing without over-swinging the other way. When wind and seas creep round to the quarter, conditions become at their worst, and some boats of apparently normal balance and rig become very wild indeed. There seems no means of determining in theory how wild a boat will be.

In getting the feel of a boat in these circumstances the skill of the helmsman is revealed by the quickness with which he anticipates the boat's movements and the judgement he shows in the amount of correcting helm he uses. To some extent the swings made by a boat as a wave train passes under her from the quarter are self-correcting. The stern is pushed down to leeward and the boat luffs up; in a moment the bow is sent down to leeward and she pays off again. To fight against these movements too violently with the helm is both fruitless and slowing for the boat. But it is rarely practicable not to fight them at all; for in the initial swing the boat may luff until all sails are lifting. This must be checked, but not to the extent that the natural swing back to leeward of the yacht is amplified to a degree that carries her off course in the other direction, so that the boat proceeds in a series of wild loops and swoops, too close to the wind at one minute, much too far off the next. It is in achieving a close mean course to the required compass course that the skill of an off-the-wind helmsman chiefly shows himself.

The qualities required are quite different from those when working to windward. I spoke above about the essentially rhythmic and dreamy nature of windward sailing. But when sailing downwind in heavy conditions it is only unremitting attention and alertness, and sometimes very violent movements of the helm, that can achieve good results. And it can be very tiring work, mentally as well as physically. An experienced helmsman can take a boat to windward for hours on end, in even heavy conditions, with strain. But frequent changes of helmsman, or at least regular if brief periods of relief for the principal helmsman, are essential when steering in heavy following seas. The concentration alone is exhausting and will inevitably be relaxed unless there are periods of rest at frequent intervals.

## HELMSMANSHIP

Those who sail a yacht well to windward do so purely by registering sensations through the hands, wrists, the seat of their pants, the skin of their face, their feet, and also through certain audible impressions. It is less a matter of alertness than of sensitivity to a number of fleeting clues all of which help to indicate how the boat is moving and what adjustments should be made. The good helmsman reacts instinctively to them; there is little conscious mental interpretation followed by action – at least when he and the boat are in perfect accord, which is a state that the best helmsman cannot maintain the whole time.

By concentration I do not mean so much having a mind preoccupied with sailing to windward, for this may be the sign of an inferior and fidgety helmsman, but rather a mind that has no other preoccupation, such as admiring the meek blue eyes of the blonde across the water and wondering where she will be this evening, or thinking hopefully of the moment when someone will think of replenishing the dry martini, or, worst of all, talking to your friends and neighbours in the cockpit. (And for that matter all people who chatter amongst themselves in the vicinity of the helmsman are not helping him.) A helmsman must be in the position that allows his trained sensory perceptions to pick up the subtle messages that the boat is all the time sending him in a stream. The better he is, the blanker, perhaps, his conscious brain. So far as possible everyone should help him to keep it blank.

For when steering to windward the helmsman is for ever adjusting the delicate relationship that exists between speed through the water and angle to the wind. The connection between pointing higher and footing faster is a complicated one and can involve the most intricate mathematical analysis when studying the results of tank tests. A mass of variables is involved in the problem: hull form, sail plan and trim, wind strength, state of the sea. The helmsman cannot study angles and speed curves in the cockpit. He solves the problem by his hands, his sense of feel, by his kinaesthetics. He becomes a computer.

And talking about hands, it is appropriate to mention one helmsman who always liked to ride a horse for an hour before steering his yacht in a race. It is also worth mentioning that analysis on shore has revealed that even the best helmsman is only spasmodic in maintaining the course that achieves the best speed made good to windward. In other words, boats are most of the time being sailed to windward a shade too fine or too full. It is probable that under sail, as in power craft, an automatic helmsman device would be better than the human hand. Experiments with one such device in the USA have indeed suggested that this is so.

Some yachts are harder to sail to windward than others. A few are so easy at moments that they become appreciably faster when the helmsman takes his hands off the helm to light a cigarette. Others – *Sceptre* was a case I believe – under certain conditions become so touchy that the helmsman finds it hard to get into any sort of accord with the yacht at all.

Those easiest to sail at their best carry slight weather helm, which at no moment becomes either uncomfortably heavy or confusingly light. The boat then responds immediately to the slightest pressure on the tiller or spoke of the wheel. She becomes an instrument under the delicate control of no more perhaps than the forefinger and thumb. When this is achieved the wind is unlikely to be much more than Force 3 and the sea slight. Then it is easiest to judge the boat's action and her fleeting responses, and the best speeds to windward may be made.

But helm responses are never constant, and in really light winds steering becomes as difficult as at any time. Many boats then carry distinct, if no great amount of, lee helm. This is anyhow bad from the point of view of speed, but it is liable to be made worse by the helmsman losing his grip and operating the helm too much. When the helm is constantly moved the amount of correction to steady the boat tends to build up. The person steering would probably be doing less harm if he left the wheel and amused himself sitting on the counter dragging the gash bucket as a drogue. Obviously, when sailing to windward, the course is never absolutely steady because the wind is constantly varying; but there is a vital difference between *steering* to the wind and *fiddling* with the helm.

\*     \*     \*

It used to be said that anyone able to handle a dinghy well could soon learn to steer a bigger ship with equal ability, whereas the reverse was not the case. I think the latter is probably true; but I doubt if the former is – not today anyhow.

Once it may have been, when quite large and heavy boats were called dinghies, and even keel craft like those of the X-class and others were put in that category. A boat of fairly heavy displacement with an outside ballast keel, even if only half-decked, reproduces at her reduced size the actions of a bigger yacht. A modern racing dinghy does not, and the utter dissimilarity of type produces two distinct styles of helmsmanship. And the technique evolved by the dinghy sailor may be nothing less than a bad habit that is hard to eradicate when applied to the helm of a heavier vessel.

The chief feature of the modern dinghy is her extreme lightness. She loses way in a moment; picks it up again equally quickly. She can only be handled by rapid and considerable helm movements capable of putting her about before a sea stops her, or of keeping her moving by a process of weaving through the seas which she lacks the power to trample down. The fact that the boat is making a more or less zigzag course from second to second does not have the serious stopping effect that it would were she a heavy-displacement yacht, for her hull is a scarcely immersed saucer of low resistance.

The situation is reversed in a bigger, ballasted keel yacht. Her weight, providing momentum, is an important element in sustaining her progress; but misused it becomes a powerful brake. The most effective way of applying the brake is to swing the yacht abruply from one course to another.

Consider what happens when the rudder is applied. We will assume, to simplify matters, that the yacht is on a downwind course. The fact that the rudder is put out to a certain angle when altering course creates a little resistance, but that of the rudder alone is a trifle. The effect of the rudder is to give the whole hull a sheer or angle of yaw – it is analogous to the angle of leeway when sailing to windward. The whole yacht, in fact, starts moving obliquely. The water pressures set up on the hull thereby, and not the rudder, ultimately turn the yacht.

But clearly this entails a great increase in resistance – something like an additional 10 per cent for each degree of yaw established. So, when a few spokes of wheel are applied, the head swings this way or that only because the hull has first been set into an oblique manner of advance, which is very much more resistful than advance straight ahead. You pay a great deal in added resistance for a few degrees of luffing up or bearing away.

John Illingworth, in a contribution to a paper read before the Institution of Naval Architects some years before the war, once described how it was always evident in the engine-room when a good quarter-master was relieved by an indifferent one, for the revolutions needed to maintain speed promptly rose. In his book, *Where Seconds Count*, he discussed the harm that big helm movements had on speed. I am less sure that his following observation is faultless: '. . . I do feel in general that it is more important to design rudders which will enable the average helmsman to steer the boat with small tiller movements rather than to go for the minimum of wetted area . . .'

This would appear to suggest that the harm comes from the helm movement in itself, whereas it lies in the movement of the whole ship in yaw, which the helm movement initiates. A small rudder must be put over farther than one of larger area to produce a given yaw angle, and hence the required degree and rapidity of alteration in course; but if the yaw angle is the same in either case, the added resistance will be also. On the other hand, perhaps an over-small rudder, because of the bigger movements needed with it, may encourage vices in the helmsman.

This is strictly beside our main theme, which has been to stress that every time the helm is moved – easy though the movement may seem, and harmless – it initiates a train of events introducing far bigger forces than those applied by the helmsman, and these tend to stop the ship. The best helmsman is the one who does not seem to be steering.

\* \* \*

We have not yet considered the position the helmsman should occupy when steering. Obviously, there can be no single answer. It depends on the point of sailing, the cockpit layout, the size and physique of the helmsman, the weight of the wind, the helm characteristics of the boat, the sails set, and, of course, on whether it is night or day, where the compass is placed and whether steering is by wheel or tiller.

Can we, out of all these variables, find a general rule to guide us initially? I think we can. The position adopted must be the one that gives the helmsman (i) the surest command of the situation and (ii) the greatest comfort. These are in order of importance. Comfort is desirable for the helmsman, but to sit down when you ought to be standing because the former position puts you in the lee of the deck-house is unjustifiable, and will not pay in the long run, even though keeping warm and dry may make you more alert.

There was a time when boats were usually sailed from up to weather. The smaller boats were generally of low freeboard, narrow and hence tender, and carried a good weight of weather helm in the tiller. To sit to leeward meant being buried in spray or solid water ( not to mention the danger of going overboard, for there were often no rails), while the weight of the helm had to be fought by the upward pressure of the bent arm, which in any strength of wind was impossibly tiring for long periods. It was considered the ideal to 'steer by the jib', but the difficulty of seeing it in small craft, the impossiblity of doing so in the larger once wheel steering had been introduced, led to the doctrine of steering by the luff of the main. With improvements in the cut of mainsails, this actually became the best sail to steer by; so, as in one of Montagu Dawson's paintings, you sat high on the weather coaming, dragging the tiller up towards you with a straight arm and the full weight of the body, and poised masterfully above the rushing seas you decided that life was fun.

The leeward position was still sometimes used; but in most yachts the first canvas to lift when sailing too fine was the luff of the mainsail. Also, in the larger craft, and except in light winds when Capt. Sycamore might steer even the 179–ton *Shamrock* with two fingers, you needed to be right on top of the wheel to control it. Pure brawn was needed to dominate the situation.

In passing, we may stop to admire for a moment the skill of that dead race of professional yacht skippers, who week after week handled the big cutters and schooners, which travelled so fast, in the crowded waters of the Solent, Clyde or Thames Estuary. Originally, they had to control these huge ships through tillers yards long, the leverage of which was augmented by tackles with several hands hauling on them. Steering a ship was then rather like conducting an orchestra. And even when the wheel became common, there was no finger-tip steering for Sycamore when the wind rose to Force 5 or so. He had to master the kicking brute under his hands; the wide expanse of deck sloped like a roof up to weather, making visibility difficult; he had to take an interest in what the mate was up to directing the sheet handling; and simultaneously he had to make delicate and often snap judgements, as the yacht moved fast with other boats near, on changes of course and tactics. It is a tribute to the skill of such men that accidents were so rare.

Life is easier today with smaller, better balanced boats, and the brute-force element in helmsmanship is relatively unimportant. But it has not disappeared, partly because the office-working helmsmen of today have not acquired that instinctive skill in deploying their strength, which was the mark of the older breed of seamen; nor have they often so much strength to deploy. The wheel of Class I ocean-racer in a Force 7 wind and seaway can cause as much damage to tender hands as rope hauling.

The first matters to decide are whether the helmsman should be (i) up to weather; (ii) down to leeward; (iii) standing or sitting. I am considering initially sailing to windward. With modern headsails the technique of sailing by the luff of the mainsail is, of course, obsolete. It can tell you nothing, and you either have to see the headsail or rely on other means of judgement. In light winds with modern headsails there seems little doubt that the leeward position and sitting down is the right one for a helmsman. It not only allows him to see the headsails and to be closely in touch with the other audible impressions which we said earlier are a helmsman's guide, but it is a relaxed position. He rests his arm along the rail, holds the helm, whether wheel or tiller, easily with one hand, and, leaning as far out as he comfortably can, is able to register as much about the motion of the boat and the action of the wind as possible.

How long, as the wind increases, this position may be maintained depends on the balance of the boat and the physique of the helmsman – also the layout of the cockpit, gearing of the wheel, and so on. What we have to remember about the leeward position is its weakness once the angle of heel and the seaway increase; there is danger of losing touch with the boat. If you are fighting with one arm and a foot to get enough weight in the wheel (and a tiller is more difficult because there is no lower spoke to kick) you cannot steer well. Also, your visibility becomes virtually negligible. If you are skipper as well as helmsman, down to lee-ward under these conditions is not the place for you. Then get up to windward and regain control.

Some people, however, with unusually strong arms and a well-developed technique in using their feet on the spokes of the wheel are able to hold this position, even in a large yacht carrying heavy helm, in quite severe conditions. If they do this, it probably remains the best position from which to steer; with the proviso that the helmsman must be asked to do nothing else. He is in a bad position from the point of view of seeing or commanding.

When steering from the weather side, some people find standing more restful than sitting, even for long periods. This is especially so if the helmsman's part of the cockpit has a radiused floor or sloping corners. But if the cockpit is well arranged and the wheel, when the helmsman is sitting well up to weather, is comfortably within reach of the outstretched arm, even heavy-weather helm can be held for long periods without undue strain.

In bad seagoing conditions, however, and particularly if sailing a little off the wind and on a compass course, with the wheel kicking and the compass being deluged from time to time, the helmsman who stands is in a better position to feel in charge of affairs. If it is lifeline weather he may find it helpful to snap the line on to the weather rail, adjusting its length so that it holds him up to windward. It takes his weight, relieving him of a great deal of the effort needed to balance himself, and, above all, it means that he does not have to use the wheel to the same extent as a support; and this allows it to be used more effectively for its main purpose of steering.

★          ★          ★

Pinching is generally regarded as the besetting fault of a helmsman when steering on the wind. It is a natural instinct, especially when

9. Reefing a Mainsail running before the wind

10. Getting 'Rapparee' to windward

*Photo: Cdr Erroll Bruce*

*Trevor Davies*

12 and 13. The lines shown on models

*British Hovercraft and Vosper Thornycroft*

racing inshore with close company. Subconsciously, unless the helmsman resists it, he becomes over-competitive in trying to point closer than his neighbours. Offshore there will usually be no neighbour to mislead; but still there is a tendency to pinch, and when this is done in a more or less heavy sea the way of a boat is killed.

Sailing inshore in calm water a few degrees closer to the wind causes less loss in speed than the same amount of luffing up when it brings big seas closer ahead, which produce pitching and a great increase in resistance. While inshore the small degree of luffing may give a better speed made good to windward; offshore the greater loss in speed through the water when sailing fine makes it profitable to sail farther, but faster and freer. In waves it is vital to keep the boat tramping.

The difficulty is, of course, to judge wisely how far off the wind to sail. It is here that helmsman's skill is the predominating factor, which is well illustrated in any one design class where marked differences in time are apparent even between experienced helmsmen on an hour's turn to windward.

Here a valuable aid to steering is provided by modern electronic instruments: the wind variation indicator and the speedometer. These aids afford the helmsman a sense of what loss or gain in speed a few degrees of luffing or paying off involve in the existing seaway and wind strength. However, while considerable refinement has been achieved with instruments it is as well to bear in mind:

(i) The difficulty with a masthead indicator of registering the *average* wind on the sail plan, which is probably around mid-height.

(ii) Every sail set receives a different apparent wind.

(iii) The effect of turbulence and gravity on the mechanism when the yacht is sailing at an angle of heel, however much these factors may be 'damped down'.

(iv) The effect of waves on wind, altering apparent wind.

I was talking about this to Adlard Coles, who was one of the first in this country to use wind indicators in his ocean-racers. He commented:

'I think electronic instruments are essential for ocean-racers. I refer in particular to the smaller classes, where all or nearly all members of the crews take a spell at the helm. First-rate experienced seamen are not necessarily first-rate racing helmsmen and vice versa. You rarely find a crew where every member could steer a boat at or near the top of a one-design class, and nowadays this is the standard required for ocean-racing as well as inshore.

But I hesitate to agree that sailing by instrument is better than the performance of a first-class helmsman, as some people say. It was interesting in the first of the new series of One Ton races at Le Havre to note that the late Mr M. H. A. van Beuningen sailed without instruments in *Hestia*, a boat which was brilliantly successful in Cowes Week regattas; and the North Sea Races. Likewise Dick Carter in *Rabbit* sailed without steering aids and, after a disappointment at Le Havre, went on to win the Fastnet Race. This shows what can be achieved without wind indicators but for all that I think instruments can at least be an aid even to the best helmsmen and are a necessity for the next best.'

It is when sailing off the wind in calm weather that steering is at its least exacting. The helmsman's one object is to keep the boat straight with – for reasons that we have seen – the minimum of helm. If inshore the course is probably being held on a mark rather than by compass. It all seems so easy that the time to chat and look around the scene appears to have arrived. For this reason crooked wakes are so often seen, when all conditions conspire to make course-keeping simple.

Once a sea gets up on the beam or quarter life becomes more exacting. In a quartering sea each wave reaches the stern first, pushing it down to leeward and causing a luff; then it reaches the bow and the boat pays off again. Under some conditions the helmsman need not fight this swing up and away. Unfortunately, the swing has effects on the sails. The spinnaker's luff may begin to curl at the end of what we may call the hydrodynamically caused luff, which is self-curing as the wave train passes, and the spinnaker and mainsail between them may produce an aerodynamic moment, which is not self-curing, tending to increase the luff.

Some boats are steadier under these conditions than others,

and length of keel has little to do with their behaviour. Certain boats can only be brought back by putting the helm hard up. When there is any weight of wind and sea, a helmsman's reaction cannot always be quick enough, nor his action, especially with wheel steering, and before he knows where he is a wave is throwing the bow off to leeward, and with the helm up the boat bears fiercely away. Chain reaction follows. In the next moment, with the helm down and wind and waves helping, she is luffing up violently. Rhythmic rolling may then occur, which means that the helmsman is not only trying to control the boat but has difficulty in staying with her.

*   *   *

Under these conditions the most important piece of rigging in the ship from the helmsman's point of view is the mainboom fore guy. Yachts on a reach in a seaway carry weather helm, sometimes fiercely, and helmsmen usually fail in the balance to counteract the luffing tendency therefore sailing high of their course. If added to this they have an anxiety about gybing all-standing, they will sail yet higher, and the boat's course will be a successions of loops and swoops up to weather. This may occur in daylight; at night the tendency is even more accentuated. Fore guys must be strong enough to give confidence.

Helmsmanship at night is in some ways a greater test than during the day. The jib cannot be seen, and when sailing to windward the burgee must be relied on, and for this purpose should be illuminated. The masthead light that does so is in an equivocal position in relation to the navigation lights that should be carried under sail; indeed, it is illegal except when shown only in the sector of the stern light.

Though compass courses mean nothing while sailing on the wind, the compass can in fact be a useful auxiliary aid when working to windward in darkness, and the helmsman anyhow has to keep his eye on it in order to estimate his mean course at the end of his trick. When other guides are lacking and the wind is fairly steady, he may check from the compass that he is not letting the boat romp – a tendency at night. As soon as he takes the wheel he should find out how the boat's head lies when she is a good full and by; then check the compass course from time to time as he steers. He must, naturally, remain alert to wind changes while doing so; also respond in the normal way to puffs and soft spots. It is desirable, too, for someone periodically to go forward and examine the jib and call back to the helmsman, enabling the latter to pick up the optimum course.

Both on and off the wind the adequacy of the compass plays a most important part in night steering. It must be clearly enough marked, both in design and size of the numerals, to be read quickly and without effort. It does seem nowadays that some compass manufacturers, in their anxiety not to make the compass light blinding, err in the opposite direction, and even when the rheostat control is at maximum there is not enough illumination. So we see helmsmen for much of their trick bowed over the compass as though about to kiss it. If a helmsman has difficulty in seeing his course he will fail to hold it accurately.

For moments at night a helmsman may find himself out of touch with his surroundings, when the compass and he are suddenly deluged, or a sudden slamming of the yacht when she drops into a hole sets up a violent oscillatory disturbance of the card. If sailing on a broad reach at the time, it is desirable to luff up a little until the situation is restored.

Another time when the sense of direction may be lost is when going about at night. The helm is put down, the head comes round, but before the headsail is sheeted again the boat is payed off excessively. This ought not to happen; the helmsman has the feel of the wind, also the burgee, to help him, but with the yacht suddenly going slower these guides become vague, and the helmsman himself may also be engaged in operating backstay levers or letting go a sheet. Before going about he should glance at the compass and, allowing about 100 degrees for the tack, note what the new course will be; then hold this until the ship is settled.

I mentioned above that there is a tendency for the helmsman to let the boat romp at night when going to windward. Ideally, in darkness as in daylight, the boat should constantly be eased up into the wind until a headsail just lifts, but the operation needs care at night, when the first lifting may not be noticed. If a helmsman luffs until he hears the headsail lifting, he not only loses way but may find the boat thrown about by an irregular sea. Here it is that the good helmsman, by night as by day, is able to show his skill, keeping apparently by instinct the boat on the edge of the wind, neither too fine nor too full.

In our notes on steering we have up to date taken the wind for granted; but here we should say something about the behaviour of the apparent wind, which is the wind in which the boat sails. Under two conditions only do the real and apparent winds come from the same direction once a vessel is moving. One is when the former is dead ahead, which is of no interest under sail; the other is when it is dead astern. But there is an important exception to the latter.

If in a following wind the boat's speed exceeds the real wind speed the apparent wind swings through a full 180 degrees and comes from dead ahead. Thus, in fluky weather, a puff may come and the boat gather way before it; then, without dropping entirely, the wind may fall off to less than the speed of the boat. Although the surface of the water may reveal that there is still a light wind blowing, the mainsail and spinnaker will collapse, and the spinnaker sheet and guy hands will probably be sworn at. There is nothing they can do about it; the situation will solve itself as the boat's speed drops again and the apparent wind flicks back 180 degrees, filling the sails once more.

If the sheet and guy hands have been fiddling with their ropes, they will probably attribute this success to their own work. The helmsman can do nothing about all this except thank the Lord that he is at the helm and not wiggle it too much.

At all times when not dead ahead or astern, the apparent wind is ahead, or closer on the bow, than the real wind. For example, if a yacht is making 6 knots in a 15-knot wind (a moderate breeze at the bottom of Force 4) blowing from 5 degrees abaft the beam, the apparent wind will come from 18 degrees ahead of the beam and will be 0·7 knot stronger than the real wind.

Here an important point, directly bearing on steering, should

be noted. A yacht's speed does not increase in proportion to the
wind's speed, but at a slower rate. As a result, an increase in wind
velocity automatically *frees* the apparent wind. Every helmsman
will know how, when sailing to windward, it is possible to point
degrees higher when a squall comes, and though this is often mis-
taken for a favourable lift it is more unlikely to be due simply to
the higher velocity of the air.

The helmsman must be alert for this swinging of the apparent
wind when sailing to windward. As soon as there are signs of a
puff he should be ready to point higher, and equally to bear away
as soon as the squall lets up. If he does not point higher he will lose
part of the opportunity for working up to windward, and if not
ready to bear away again he will be headed, lose speed, and waste
time getting the boat moving again.

When sailing with the wind on the beam, however, the helmsman employs the reverse technique, which may seem surprising.
He should bear away to a squall and luff to a lull. Thereby he
can keep the boat moving well in the freer winds of the puffs;
but, what is more important, it gives him scope to luff to the
lighter airs of the lulls and so increase the apparent wind speed
and also bring the yacht on to the course which, for modern
craft, is her most efficient in light and moderate winds, with the
wind some 45 degrees off the bow.

# 5

# DESIGNERS
# AND DESIGNING

## THE PROFESSION OF YACHT DESIGN

When Phineas Pett received instructions from the Lord High-Admiral in 1604 to '. . . build in all haste a miniature pleasure ship' he became the first English yacht architect. He was, of course, a shipbuilder of some repute, and yachts were a side-line; though a not unimportant one, for his clients were various members of the gay House of Stuart. The King and many of his family had taken delightedly and light-heartedly to the new sport of sailing for the fun of it, and this first yacht designer therefore had the most influential patronage.

In the dawn of modern yachting, which shone a little wanly at first on the early Victorian scene, the design of the numerous coastal traders and fishermen was the work of men who were primarily builders, and it was they who turned their hands to yachts when the demand arose. But their livelihood came from their small yards; they designed simply as a part of the function of building. Of this breed was the Fife dynasty, founded by 'Ould Wull', who turned shipwright from wheelwright early in the nineteenth century, and whose son and grandson brought, by their yachts, fame to the little village of Farlie by the Clyde.

Some of the greatest designers remained proprietors of yards, which expanded and became small shipyards of some importance. Design work was certainly more than a hobby to them, and their creativeness was the net which fished contracts for their building establishments; but they were usually the first to agree that they had, fortunately, a yard for a livelihood, and were not called on to live by the pencil. But gradually yacht design became to many an occupation apart. It was withdrawn from the ken of the shipwright, as a few centuries earlier the practice of architecture had been dissociated from the work of the mason and master builder. Yacht design became a specialized branch of naval architecture.

H

And something else too; for many of its ablest practitioners were not, and are not, fully equipped naval architects. It became, and remains today, a slightly esoteric occupation having more in common with the fine arts than with the work of the specialists who draw parts of ships in the offices of the great shipbuilding concerns.

This was all very fine during the four lavish decades before 1914, when yacht designers lived in the flush of a liberal patronage; and it was not too bad during the twilight of this period which lingered between the wars. Even then, however, the advice of sensible people to parents who were considering yacht design as a career for their expensively educated children was identical in import to that of Noel Coward to Mrs Worthington. What are we to think of the profession today, when designers' patrons – individually rich men – have become rare, and such patrons of the other arts as public bodies and associations cannot replace them?

If a yacht designer is to get an adequate return for his labour he must either design big yachts, or have numerous boats built from each of his designs for smaller craft. We must understand an economic fact of yacht design – that a 20-tonner may cost more than four times as much as a 5-tonner, but that the amount of work entailed in her design will not be four times as great. A yacht designer has not the time to draw four 5-tonners instead of one 20-tonner. It takes no longer to draw the lines of a 20-tonner, and it may even be done more quickly since less delicate compromise is needed. The sail plan of either entails much the same amount of work. The construction plan of the larger yacht will take longer, but not four times as long, and the same applies to the drawing of the accommodation.

As for the supervision of the construction, we may say that this will occupy more time in the case of the larger boat, but here we may well be wrong for so much depends on the individual circumstances of the case. There is another point: evidence does not suggest that the owner of a 5-tonner is less exacting than the owner of a 20-tonner; he may be more so, and require as great an expenditure of time on correspondence, telephone calls, and conferences.

The designer is faced with a further difficulty today. There was a time when he had done his job once he had provided the hull lines and a table of offsets, a construction drawing with the scantlings written thereon, and a sail plan and rigging list. Details were 'according to usual practice'. Now every tang, every deck eyebolt, every cabin drawer, seems to need its separate drawing. A 5-tonner today may emerge from a bigger mass of draughtsmanship than an America's Cup challenger of the last century; and those with experience of detail drawing know well how long it takes, what a weariness it is, and how it may smother creativeness.

It is, of course, well known that the real artist will let his wife and children starve before he will sacrifice his vocation. He may even sacrifice his own before-dinner gin to the cause. Financially the yacht designer is helped, assuming his fee to be in proportion to the price of the boat, by the tremendous increase in the cost per ton of modern construction. Since this increase is largely a reflection of the higher wages now paid to artisans, the yacht designer is in the happy position, unlike most professional men and artists, of gaining something out of this century of the common man. But it is not enough to compensate for what he has lost in the patronage of those who can afford large and expensive yachts. Whether the yacht designer can secure his economic foundation in the present age, and so ensure his survival, is at least open to doubt.

Yet, happily, the demand for his services continues. At the end of the war, and during the first years of peace, many people assured us with cold-blooded delight that the day of the mass-produced boat had arrived, that every soul in this land of the free would be enabled to take to the water in some sort of craft, whether cooked in an oven, cast in glass, or stuck together with glue and pins by ignorant girls in mammoth factories. Obviously the day of the designer was over. A single design would suffice for a few thousand boats.

Yet designers remain busy – if poor.

## HONOURS AND YACHT ARCHITECTS

You may or may not agree with the quaint, many-runged ladder of the English Honours system. It certainly does make it necessary for some pretty delicate distinctions to be made; such as whether it is more meritorious to have sung 'I Belong to Glasgie' to many audiences for many years, or to have designed the warships that saved the nation and Empire in the 1914–18 War. In this case the two achievements were judged to be of precisely equal merit. Sir Harry Lauder and Sir Phillip Watts both died as knights. Only peerages, of course, were good enough for the profiteers in 1918.

However, everyone likes recognition for their achievements, and as we have a complicated system of badges and awards for the purpose, it is appropriate to make it as reasonable as such a genuinely difficult business may be made. This is Argus's attempt to improve the Constitution, undertaken on behalf of all those who have created our ships, and particularly our yachts.

To the world of naval architecture, considering the whole profession of which yacht architecture is the branch carrying the brightest and most glamorous bloom, I do not think that one, even barony, the lowest order of nobility, has ever been offered in all our history; which is odd when one considers that for some centuries the might of Empire (let alone our island security and prosperity) depended upon the quality of our war and merchant ships no less upon the ability with which they were handled.

You might find yourself with a coronet for brewing beer; you might even do so for *building* ships if your yard was big enough; but if you just *designed* them, no coronet for you. A Director of Naval Construction, in former years a man holding one of the most crucial and exacting defence posts in the Empire that was, habitually received a K.C.B. for sometimes many years of office; a Lord Mayor of London enters the Baronetage after one year of office, and his son and his son's son unto the end of virility will trail his glory from generation to generation.

We have prided ourselves upon being a great maritime power, but we have shown precious little pride in the men who created the ships which made us one. Sweden, with what seems to me a shrewder sense of values, raised Frederik Chapman, the great naval architect of the eighteenth century and of pure British descent, to the nobility of his adopted country.

All this being so, we cannot be surprised that yacht architects have rarely figured in even humbler massed orders. You might earn a K.C.B. for removing a Prime Minister's appendix, but Watson did not receive even an M.B.E. for designing a King's yacht; yet that yacht – the unforgotten cutter *Britannia* – was the glory and the figurehead of British yachting for decades while Britain was the greatest yachting nation on earth. (I believe, though it is a piece of history I cannot substantiate, that King Edward VII wished to honour George Watson, but advice prevailed against it with so many others pushing at the door.)

For decades, too, the late Charles E. Nicholson carried the banner of British yacht design and construction over the international scene; and in foreign countries the art and industry of British yachting a not inconsiderable section of British life – was personified in that quiet, modest gentleman. It is not too much to claim that at some time in his career the best yachts in the world of every type – power, sail, cruising, racing – were to his design and constructed in his yard; and the yard played an important part in two World War efforts. While comedians, jockeys, cartoonists, manufacturers of corsets and shoals of back-bench M.P.s who had warmed their seats for the requisite number of years, became knights and baronets, a grateful government awarded Charles E. Nicholson, very late in his life, an O.B.E. As one once-well-known and, as it happens, noble yachtsman, said to me: 'I wish he'd sent it back'.

Today, when the fountain of honours deluges such broad acres, we may expect better things for our yacht designers and builders. So it is not only for personal reasons of friendship but on the broadest principle of making honours as sensible as possible that I welcome the C.B.E. given to Peter Du Cane in the New Year's Honours List. It is something. He is, of course, a versatile man – the creator, out of a backyard boatyard, of a shipyard that built the majority of our MTBs for our wartime coastal forces; he is an author and a lecturer; a seaman, and as it happens an airman too; and he combines a pure-blue technician (not only a naval architect but a Commander (Engineering), R.N.) with the flair of the artist – which is unusual.

His work as a naval architect and shipbuilder has cut deep into the world of yachting, though he has never touched sailing-craft. Before the war he was a pioneer in the field of fast runabouts of that period, which have proliferated into the high-speed craft of today; and it was most apt that *Tramontana*, to his design and his yard's construction, should have won the *Daily Express* International Power Boat Race in 1962.

In *Mercury* he produced the fastest seagoing yacht in the world, and incidentally established an entirely new form of yacht beauty in the process. He designed Sir Malcolm Campbell's *Bluebird II* which held the World's Water Speed Record between 1938 and 1950. Also he designed several large ocean-going motor yachts of moderate speed, such as the 218-ton T.M. *Deianeira* in 1951. And he has made many unhappy stomachs in the world of motor yachting happier by extending the principle of using activated fins for roll damping from the biggest ships to small craft of down to about 50 ft overall. In this also he was a pioneer.

May he prove to be a pioneer too in making the dedicated profession of ship and yacht design fashionable enough to receive its share of conventional honours.

## DESIGN – ART AND SCIENCE

An experienced designer's opinions of his fellow practitioners are likely to be interesting – and sometimes scurrilous too. But it was more than this natural interest which drew me to Clinton Crane's remarks on William Fife in his biography. 'I admired', writes Mr Crane, 'Fife's perfecion of form . . . engineering is relatively easy to learn . . . but I doubt whether any amount of teaching would enable a man to model a statue like Praxitales, Phidias or Michelangelo.' Fife, Clinton Crane writes elsewhere, had an eye for form, and it is clear that in his opinion it was a better eye than Nathaniel Herreshoff's, in spite of this designer's wide range of genius and his habit of deriving hull lines by carving a model, for which practice a singular feeling for form is necessary.

Now we have here a familiar view, though one which gains value through being expressed by a designer having high technical qualifications, with nothing of the inspired amateur about him, and with experience of designing racing yachts stretching from little skimming dish raters at the end of the last century to 12-Metres and 'J' Class boats in this. Clinton Crane places a high value upon instincts and artistic flair.

Traditionally the design of sailing-yachts, and particularly of their hull shape, is believed to be mainly an art. Words such as 'finely formed', 'beautiful', even 'inspired' fall readily from the pens of those who describe the waterlines, diagonals and the various other projections. which delineate a yacht's shape on a piece of paper. A designer, handling his battens and weights at his drawing-table as he portrays the shape of the hull which he has conceived in his mind, is regarded as a kind of mystical cross between a sorcerer and a poet.

This philosophy of design is not uncontested. The late Dr K. S. M. Davidson is well known for the work he did at the Stevens Institute, Hoboken, in developing the technique of tank testing for sailing-craft. It is possibly true to say that the superiority of America in the design of 'J' Class boat, of 12-Metres and 6-Metres – those classes in which the quality of hull design really is tested, which is not the case in ocean racing – owes at least as much to him as to that brilliant designer Olin Stephens who worked so closely with him. And Professor Davidson has said: 'I have never held much with the occult implications of those who pin their faith on the mystery of the "subtlety of lines" in any sort of hydro-dynamic designing.' Sorcerers and poets in fact were not for him. He regarded a yacht producing a hull shape in the same light as he would an aeroplane draughtsman drawing a wing shape – a surprisingly similar process in solid geometry as it happens.

I have often felt that the process of drawing a set of hull lines – an intensely enjoyable task whether undertaken professionally or as a hobby – is exaggerated in importance. It is a skill but not a major creative frenzy. The important *design* work, which will determine all the salient features and characteristics of a yacht, is done when the leading dimensions, the displacement, the form of the midship section, the longitudinal position of the centre of buoyancy, and the form of the keel, are chosen in the earliest stages of the design.

To arrive at the right choice in each case is a species of genius, the result of an infinely painstaking study, extending over years, of the way of the sailing-boat and of the hydrodynamic laws governing her behaviour. But once the decisions have been made they may be expressed clearly enough on the back of an envelope for the draughtsman who knows a fair from an unfair line to translate them into a set of hull-lines.

I believe that Charles E. Nicholson rarely drew a set of hull-lines fully with his own hands. Having chosen the leading dimensions and drawn a deckline, load waterline, and profile, the lines were handed for completion to his staff, after which he would suggest modifications where desirable. But I have also heard the story of how one evening, finding that after a week, work on a set of hull-lines was slow and not as he wished, he brought a clean sheet of paper home with him and returned to the yard next morning with the drawing faired and completed.

\*      \*      \*

It is always a good thing to clarify what we mean by the words we use. Frequently, as the philosophers know, we then find we have not said what we thought. What is the difference between the artist and the scientist? The artist, within the range of this discussion, is presumably one who arrives at a certain shape through an innate, irrational (in the sense that he is not guided consciously by data and reasoning) feeling of 'rightness' in that shape. This sense of form is purely aesthetic. So it was that the dome of St Peter's rose against the Italian sky in glory. The scientist, however, produces a shape because reason and the application of the relevant data lead him inexorably to it.[1] He has no freedom of choice. The aeroplane designer chooses a wing section and plan by studying the aerodynamic properties revealed in wind tunnels of numerous different types of aerofoil. If there is any flair – or artistry – involved, it enters only to bridge a gulf where ignorance prevails. It is my belief that the smaller the areas of ignorance that the

[1] It ought to be added that the dome, including its shape, was fundamentally an engineering, not an artistic, product.

sailing yacht architect has to cross, guided by no better compass than his aesthetic instincts, the better the yacht will be.

This does not mean that the yacht will necessarily win races. Ought we not to realize that we tend to judge the quality of a yacht's basic design by a most unscientific criterion – her race-winning ability? I would suggest that a more rational parameter for assessing performance would be not the lines on the designer's board, but (i) the amount of money spent on sails, gear and hull finish; (ii) the trouble the owner takes in getting the best crew; (iii) the ability of the helmsman.

Given equality in (i), (ii) and (iii) between two boats, then the winner will be the one designed by the man who knows most about the hydrodynamics of sailing, who has the best and most plentiful data, not the one who relies on the sculptor's instinct.

It is sometimes said: 'No yacht designer worth his salt is anything but an artist . . .', a statement meaning that any yacht architect who attempts to apply data and conscious analysis of cause and effect to his work is suspect. What is needed is 'a complete understanding of, and sympathy for "line" '. So we are led to believe that the same species of gift that created the lovely, innocent and relaxed attitude of Copenhagen harbour's mermaid is needed to produce a good sailing-yacht's hull.

The professional naval architect's design office prefers people who can face a coefficient calmly, and preferably those who know more mathematics than addition and subtraction. For obvious reasons, the design of sailing-yachts is in a more primitive state than that of engine-driven vessels, while the problem they offer is in many ways more complex. So a designer has quite a lot of guessing to do.

The untutored draughtsman who has mastered the technique of using weights and splines and drawing a set of hull-lines – an ability not possessed by many otherwise good draughtsmen and lacking too in some naval architects, but one with slight hydro-dynamic significance – may produce most successful sailing-yachts because the fortunes of weather and racing are scattered at random, and excellence of rigging, gear and handling can easily offset mediocre hull-lines. The difference between the excellent hull and the only moderately good is perhaps a few seconds per mile. A bad helmsman or tactician can lose this time in as many minutes, and a snarl up with a spinnaker will lose minutes not seconds.

I would amend the statement quoted above to: 'Every yacht designer worth his salt is a scientist and an engineer, but to achieve excellence he must be an artist too, so that his creations may be beautiful as well as good.'

Fife creates the beauty of *Evenlode*, Giles the grace of a motor-yacht like *Freelander*, out of their abundant gifts as artists. Nothing but the artist can yet produce a beautiful yacht. But except by luck – the off-the-cuff chance – only the good hydrodynamist can produce the best basic sailing hull of which we are capable today.

## DESIGN – SCIENCE AND SENSE

Only the very simple-minded imagine that science is incompatible with common sense. Science is organized knowledge, and as such is more likely to help common sense than knowledge that is not organized.

For many years seamen have described a ship as 'smelling the land' in referring to the tendency of a vessel to sheer away from shoal water when steaming parallel with a submerged bank. Skilful ships' masters have made use of this almost human characteristic of certain ships by allowing them to have their own way when nosing up a narrow channel, giving them the freedom of their own initiative in sheering from side to side and thus holding the deep water under the keel. No doubt the simplest sailors on board were awed by this manifestation of the ship's apparently human sense; so that for them one more element was added to the great body of ship mysticism. The scientist explained the matter in terms of hydrodynamic laws, of pressures, Bernoulli, and equations.

The ships' masters were men of practical common sense. The seamen were mystics – for it is said that mysticism begins where knowledge ends. The scientist took the knowledge that to the seamen was uncanny, to the master useful and convenient, and put it in its true place in the pattern of phenomena. Thus science is made.

Once, when those wonderful playthings of days gone, the J-Class boats, were of interest, some of the best brains not simply in yacht design but in the whole science of hydrodynamics, occupied themselves with the problem of the best length of boat to suit this rule. Should she be 80 ft on the waterline, or 87 ft or something in between? It took roughly speaking from the *Enterprise* of 1930 to the *Ranger* of 1937 for the Americans to learn that the answer was 87 ft.

The argument was fought with resistance curves, plottings on logarithmic scales, and treatise of great erudition by many very clever men. Whilst the discussion was at its height L. Francis Herreshoff, himself the designer of the J-Boat, *Whirlwind*, broke out of this *haute cuisine* of yacht design and came down to the common stew-pot. It was worth noting, he pointed out, that the success of recent J-Class yachts was in an exact mathematical proportion to the number of sails delivered to each by the sailmaker. This set a new note in the arguments, and Mr C. P. Burgess who designed for the J-Class Enterprise her duralumin mast, agreed that ' . . . there are a great many variables which influence the speed of yachts. Perhaps one of the most important and least regarded is what the skipper had for dinner the night before'.

Clearly this was a long way from the logarithmic plotting of resistance curves, though hardly less important. And no less scientific. It obviously had its place – and a significant one – in the pattern of phenomena. It still has. And so, of course, has the interpretation of complex curves. And so too, perhaps, has mysticism. For Larent Giles has confessed of yacht design that ' . . . we only know the rudiments – the rest is conjecture'.

## K. S. M. DAVIDSON

With the death of Professor K. S. M. Davidson, yacht architecture has lost its greatest theoretician. He was only sixty and as agile in mind as ever. And he died at a time when the fullest fruit of his work was appearing. He had been serving as a scientific adviser on the staff of SHAPE, but he is best known to us as the Director of the Stevens Institute Experimental Towing Tank, Hoboken, and the investigator who devised the first method of effectively tank testing the hulls of sailing yachts.

Such activities may seem remote from the yachtsman interested primarily in maintaining, sailing and living on board the small ship of his own, but it is not only the more expensive inshore or offshore racing yachts that profited from his studies. Sometimes it may be forgotten how much the art of design has improved in the years since 1936. It showed itself in the fact that when four designers who had never had a 12-Metre built from their drawings before produced designs for an America's Cup challenger, their conceptions proved in the tank to be notably superior to the pre-war 12-Metres. But it shows itself too nearer home for most people than in the production of Cup racers. The cruiser and cruiser-racer of 5 to 10 tons is today a sailing and seagoing machine of a calibre hardly known in 1939. And this is attributable, at least partly, to the apparently recondite work of Davidson.

He was, in fact, a most unprofessorial kind of person in manner, perhaps because he was also a yachtsman of experience. He was happy seagoing. He sailed with Rod Stephens in *Stormy Weather* on the famous 3,000-mile passage from Breton Cove to Bergen, and Stephens wrote shortly afterwards: 'To maintain the technical calibre of our watch we had Professor Davidson. Ken as a watch-mate, or anything else, could not be improved on, except for the possible elimination of that perpetually precarious 1-in. ash on his cigarette and his unfailing neglect to replace the barber-chair cover after each use. . . . But what a blessing to have a shipmate on whom you can blame any of the faults the other watch may discover! And better still if he can have the ability to work sights more quickly than the navigators, to make and explain weather maps and ice charts from the radio operator's code, and to swear by all that's holy that he prefers fog and cold to sun when the passage is 85 per cent foggy.'

I met him for dinner the evening before he left England for the last time, when he went out to Turkey and fell ill there. There were times when another Davidson appeared, not the scientist or the seaman, but the poet that sustained both. He had a love for and knowledge of English poetry that showed itself in an unerring accuracy of quotation. It might be Shakespeare. He was one of the few people who to my ear could quote him tolerably. It might be brilliant, mock-heroic nonsense from 'The Hunting of the Snark'. It might be Humpty Dumpty:

> 'I sent a message to the fish:
> I told them "This is what I wish".
>
> The little fishes of the sea
> They sent an answer back to me.
>
> The little fishes' answer was
> "We cannot do it, sir, because —"'

He had an ear for music that was not surprising when one had appreciated his sensitivity to the music of language, his ability to raise the subtle evocative power of words.

His classic technical paper on yachts appeared before the Society of Naval Architects and Marine Engineers, New York, in 1936, under the title of 'Some Experimental Studies of the Sailing Yacht'. He said at the outset: 'It was clear in 1932, when these studies were begun, that previous model tests of yacht hulls had failed to produce useful design information.' This had led him to examine and explain why, in the past, small models, as opposed to those of 15 ft or more in length, which were usual for testing ships but were impractically large for yachts, had produced erroneous results. His conclusions were of the greatest importance to general naval architecture, for the use of small models, little more than 3 ft long, allowed the model testing technique to be extended over a wider range, and today much experimental work is done at this scale.

His next step was to examine the peculiarities of the sailing problem in detail. He was able, as he said, ' . . . to dispose at once of any idea that the upright resistances are a sufficient measure of the general ability of a yacht hull under sail', and he devised the dynamometer, by means of which the leeway angle and the lateral forces resulting from it were taken into account. This entailed measuring the forces produced by a rig, and the well-known

*Gimcrack* coefficients were produced. In the discussion on the paper, Olin Stephens said: 'I have had sufficient confidence to make use of these tests and accept their verdict in regard to the new "J" boat on which I am working with Starling Burgess, as well as a number of smaller boats of both racing and cruising type.' Thus was the triumphant America's Cup defender *Ranger* born. Her outstanding ability was due partly to her unusual hull form, partly to the choice of her leading dimensions. Both were sufficiently unusual to have been unacceptable but for the technique of tank testing, which provided assurance in the decision.

## ORANGES AND LEMONS

'Which end of the pear?' people were asking each other with furrowed brows some years ago. They meant, is it better for a boat to have a blunt bow and sharp stern or vice versa? A huge and highly qualified consensus of opinion decided it was better to incline towards bluntness forward rather than aft.

Not too blunt, mark you, but blunt enough. And you could hardly be too fine aft. Think of the Dutch botters – rich, bosomy bows and hardly any sterns at all. And they have survived for centuries. An extreme example perhaps, but suggestive . . . At the least, bows and sterns should be almost the same shape, and no nonsense with fine bows and full sterns.

When *Circe* was the loveliest 6-Metre on either side of the Atlantic, and some believed the fastest too, her thin stern and tapering counter were admired by all. 'Sculpturally lovely, technically right,' said an eminent designer. 'Fill out your bows, fine down your sterns, and you will become a great architect like me.' For many years everyone agreed with this.

*Sceptre* was very like *Circe* (not surprisingly, being produced by the same architect, David Boyd) but forward she was even more so, with a bow as blunt as a bulldog's nose. 'That bow of *Sceptre's*,' said the eminent architect, 'is a stroke of genius. And the stern is a honey too – like *Circe's*.' And he blew a kiss into the air.

Almost everyone agreed. After all, it was obvious that bow and stern should match one another as nearly as possible, and that the bow, going first, should be nice and bouncy. Harmony is all. Think of the Vikings' ships – almost double-ended. *That* shape has survived for centuries.

So Charlie Nicholson produced a series of uncommonly fast yachts, very blunt forward, very fine aft, and we all knew why they went so well; and were able to explain it to our readers. Harmony is everything, and very convenient as well. You just designed a bow (or stern) and handed it to a stooge to copy for the stern (or bow). This was the way to win designing competitions too.

American centreboarders like *Finisterre* were disconcerting, so very full aft, so knife-like forward. 'Do you know,' said an earnest and experienced observer of yacht design gazing sadly at his drawing-table, 'that the heeled shape of Olin Stephens' *Finisterre* sailing *backwards* is almost exactly like one of C. A. Nicholson's SCO–Ds sailing *forwards?* If only they didn't both sail so well we might know where we were.'

*Sceptre* was disconcerting too.

So theory had to pick up its skirts and think. It had been silly to believe that bows and sterns should be alike. After all, one goes in front and the other follows after. Different purposes require different shapes. Think of the Yorkshire cobles and American cat boats; and those shapes have survived for centuries. 'Discord is all,' said the eminent designer.

Thus it happened that David Boyd gave *Sovereign* and *Kurrewa V* stems with a cutting edge from head to keel and harsh, flat sterns. And now we have to explain *that* to our readers. It makes life hard for us when the most eminent designers put their ideas into reverse.

And now, bless us, they've gone mad about rigs as well.

'Keep the mast straight and stop worrying about hull form,' said the eminent designer. '*That* is the secret of sailing speed.' A chorus of approval greeted him, and every textbook and right thinker helped him with moral support and equations. They were happy days when at least one important job on board could be done lying flat on your back – at the foot of the mast mesmerizing that suffering stick into straightness. Happy days too with monkey wrenches on the rigging screws, every bit of wire a fiddle string, and the yacht springing violent leaks as the bow and stern rose and threatened to meet at the masthead. Then we knew we were really getting somewhere; and the owner was charmed.

It was tiresome when the Dragon and Finn people, and other outsiders who couldn't keep their masts straight anyhow, began to *make* them bend. But they were small craft with peculiar likes and dislikes. Ocean-racers and big craft must have straight masts. We all knew our Illingworth by heart.

Then *Constellation*, a new American 12-Metre by Olin Stephens, a defender of the *America's* Cup, was given a flexible mast. How willy we all were to think that masts should be straight, our stays twanging. For centuries the great old sailors used masts like fishing-rods and their stays hung in bights. 'Looseness is all,' says the eminent designer. 'Lets have lots of give everywhere.'

## ROBBING THE ARCHITECT

Occasionally I have sniped at the contemporary secretiveness of naval architects over their drawings, particularly their unwillingness to publish hull-lines, which contrasts with the attitude common in the decade before the war. There are a number of exceptions, but a designer's policy usually progresses thus: early in his career he publishes with the utmost readiness as fully and as often as possible; then, reputation established, the curtain falls on much of his work, and he releases only sail plans and general arrangements of his designs. I believe that sometimes an architect even publishes spurious lines and intentional mistakes on both drawings and in data. Perhaps in the past I have been less than fair to the architects' point of view in this matter, and some redress is called for.

There are many yachts sailing at this moment that are based wholly or in part upon published designs of an architect of which the designer has no knowledge and for which he has received no royalty. Occasionally chance may bring a case to light, but the legal situation is difficult. A number of slight modifications in a design may make it difficult for an architect to prove his copyright, and, anyhow, the process is fraught with all the expenses and uncertainties, all the weary, time-consuming palaver that makes the massive dignity and majesty of the march of justice towards its appointed and not always satisfactory destination. The law is a dangerous crutch for the innocent poor; and yacht architects rarely qualified to be classed as rich. Authors, who are poor too, do at least have powerful, widely recognized laws of copyright to protect them. They reach their public through the medium of publishers who are not only shrewd businessmen, but well enough breeched to look after their own and their author's interests in the case of a flagrant violation of copyright that demands legal action. The yacht architect has none of these advantages.

Here is a true story, the experience of a well-known practising British designer: The lines plan, construction, general arrangement and sail plan of one of his yachts was published. A builder beyond our shores had the drawings 'blown up' by photostat to a scale of one inch to the foot and proceeded to lay off the lines and use the construction plan for building. The architect was told that a yacht to his design was being built at the yard of 'X', which interested him very much. Supporting evidence came to hand in a photograph of the yacht under construction. The very process of the stealing builder was now used to undo him (for I am pleased to say that *this* story at least has a happy ending). The photograph showed the plans of the boat pinned to a board and standing conveniently propped up on the bench beside the partially planked yacht. This photograph was in turn 'blown up', and lo – there could be read on the photostat on the board the title of the publication from which the plans had been photographed. The architect wrote to the yard saying that he was interested to learn that a yacht to his design was under construction at their yard. He showed polite interest in the progress of the work. He enclosed his bill for royalties. I should like to think that he doubled the number he first thought of, but as this story is true I must not add embellishments. Shortly afterwards he received his cheque.

But justice only rarely is the outcome of such affairs; though occasionally poetic justice emerges. Another architect once had a published design containing deliberate mistakes copied and used for construction, mistakes and all. But along our coasts and, perhaps more commonly, along the coasts of far-away lands, practising designers of today have yachts more or less to their designs of which they have not heard, or perhaps of which they have heard but of which too they cannot by any practicable process establish paternity.

However, the publication of drawings is not the only source of leakage. When a yacht is under construction drawings become liberally scattered about the place. When the work is finished the fate of the prints is rarely watched. They are capable of walking far. There is another true story of plans which were left lying around after the building of a yacht was complete; and in due time they were not lying about any longer. Some years afterwards an interesting class of boat appeared elsewhere. The design had been judiciously modified. There was no doubt who its daddy was, though it would have been hard pressed to say when it had last seen its father. This story has no happy ending. For how much alteration must you make in the design of someone else to convert it into your own original work?

In any form of art the best practitioners are usually those saturated in the best work of those who preceded them. Influence is inevitable. In literature the more subtle forms of plagiarism are rampant. It was not only Homer of whom it is true that:

> 'They knew 'e stole; 'e knew they knowed.
> They didn't tell, nor make a fuss,
> But winked at 'Omer down the road,
> And 'e winked back – the same as us.'

Shakespeare, had there been international laws of copyright in his day, would have been sued from Heaven by Herodotus. I once amused myself comparing Herodotus's fine passages on Cleopatra gliding in her barge to meet her Antony with Shakespeare's. Words, whole phrases and sentences have been lifted by Shakespeare from the English translation of Herodotus, on which he relied for the story. The fact that in the process he converted good, firm prose into poetry that can tear the heart out of all but aesthetic morons does not alter the fact that Bill, like 'Omer, pinched the best ideas of other people, and passed them off as his own, with or without a wink. (Often without.) And so we are blessed with

'. . . the oars were silver
Which to the tune of flutes kept stroke, and made
The water which they beat to follow faster,
As amorous of their strokes . . .'

We must agree, then, that every yacht architect, like every creative worker in any sphere, cannot entirely possess his work once it has gone out into the world; and the greater the work the greater the likelihood is of the world taking it to be common property. But at some indeterminate point pure stealing begins.

It is unadulterated when published plans are enlarged photographically and used as working dragings. It is only a little less so when the drawings of another are used as a basis of a design in which only details are altered, the profile modified, the accommodation adjusted, and the outcome passed off as a new design by someone else. On the other hand, an architect has to accept the fact that successful features that he incorporates in his designs may be adopted by others, and his consolation must be that he, too, once learned from his predecessors.

\*     \*     \*

I was once looking at drawings in an architect's office, and as we worked through the sheets the inevitable question was often asked and usually answered in the same way: 'Would you let me publish that set of lines?' 'I would not.' 'Then what about that set?' 'No! Definitely not!' Earlier the architect had said: 'You know that hull-lines are always available for you to examine here and make notes about, whenever you wish.'

The stealing of architects' work as a result (i) of publication or (ii) of the working drawings held by the owner and builder during construction going adrift is an activity that the pressure of public opinion might do something to suppress. I have been amazed to find how common the practice has become in certain parts of the world, how widely known it is, and how calmly accepted.

Another architect sent me the photostat of a letter from a yachtsman in another country in which the following observations appear: '*Blank* was one of the few of our yachts on which a design fee was paid! *Nine out of ten*, I am sorry to say, are built from blown-up published plans. *No wonder some of them are a little odd.*' He goes on to say: 'The Americans suffer worst in this respect – Sparkman & Stephens would have a fit if they knew how many of their designs are afloat in these waters – but there are quite a few British ones around too.'

The comment about Sparkman & Stephens is of particular interest. So far as I know, this firm now never publishes hull-lines, so the oddness of reputably Stephens designs may partially at least be accounted for. One could only wish that the results were odd enough, aesthetically and at sea, to discourage stealing.

The temptations to steal designs is strong. For, let us face it, architects' fees are quite an impressive item in the total cost of a new yacht. A friend of mine is building a new boat, as it happens to a Stephens' design, and the fee he is paying (the yacht is being constructed without architect's supervision) franky disconcerted me when I heard it. But this is partly due to the inevitably higher price of things American.

However, even British architects' fees are to not be lightly shouldered, especially if they can be evaded. People with a little knowledge may know enough to realize that most even new designs from the office of an experienced architect are derived from earlier designs. The hull-lines are probably taken directly, with only the slightest adjustments, from former proved boats of the same type. The main alterations are likely to be in the accommodation and perhaps the rig to suit the latest customer's requirements. Then, afterwards, this new design will be used as the basis for others. Knowing this, the ignorant will say: 'It is not worth the price.'

Those same people will pay a well-known surgeon (because they can't get his services otherwise) a great sum for an operation that may take a few hours and perhaps half a dozen short visits following it. Total time involved for the surgeon perhaps four hours, to which with generosity we will add another four hours to cover the time he has spent thinking and worrying over the case while not actually attending it. So he may earn for an eight-hour-day's work appreciably more than a hundred pounds. The implications in this argument are clearly misleading, but they illustrate a similar falsity in the approach of many people to the fees of the yacht architect.

True, if successful, the income he derives per hour of work, after covering the salary of his designing draughtsmen and overheads, may not be despicable. But success has only been the outcome of years of experience, his profession is desperately insecure, and unless he has a private income he ought (though it is usually impossible) to save. Also, what is meant by 'hours of work'? Yacht designing (those who write habitually about yachts are related to architects in this respect) is a consuming activity that keeps you in a small, all-pervasive world. Life cannot be divided neatly into the compartments of 'office' and 'out-of-the-office'. You live, more or less, in the office or in bed; for most of your friends are probably yachtsmen, your clubs yacht clubs, your sport sailing.

The yacht architect earns the money he makes in a harder way than the average successful professional in other fields. Aware of this, designers are sometimes perhaps a little over-anxious to discover and complain about copying of their work – and sometimes by other architects. Three yacht designers in the last few months have complained to me, with examples ready of what they regarded as close copying of their work by three other designers. In one case certainly the degree of similarity, down to the position of slight points of contraflexure in the lines plan, was remarkably close.

But this is beyond the immediate scope of what we are saying here; which is the stealing of designs or partial designs by the unskilled for construction use without payment of fees. The law can do little, I believe, and only public opinion can help.

# 6

# READING THE LINES

14. Stem, keel and frame amidships in position

15. Most of the laminated frames in position

16. The bottom planked, dowels not yet trimmed off

*Photographs 14, 15, 16, 17 and 18 taken at Berthon, Lymington by Dalgety Public Relations*

17. Topsides completed and bottom being caulked

18. Deck being laid

19. Cold moulding a hull at Souters of Cowes

*F. A. Squibb*

## READING THE LINES

To represent exactly within the two dimensions of a sheet of paper the three dimensional and vigorously curved form of a yacht or ship is a quite involved process of solid geometry. This Lines Plan as it is called is the basis of scientific naval architecture. By means of it the naval architect is able to invent and subsequently convey to others pretty accurately the shape of a solid form before it has ever been solidified.

Not surprisingly, the technique eluded men for a long time, as did the different technique of perspective in painting, and centuries were needed to perfect the processes of geometrical projection by means of which the shapes of yachts are now portrayed regularly in the yachting journals. To make a lines drawing is skilled work for which not only training but flair is needed, and many otherwise excellent designing draftsmen and architects lack the latter.

It is often found that in the design office of a big shipyard only one or two people are adroit in preparing a set of lines, and they may not be the most knowledgeable or experienced naval architects. But they are valuable people for the experienced architect to have around. He knows what shape of ship is required; the draftsmen with the flair is able to express it readily by using the geometrical processes involved in producing a set of hull-lines.

There is a powerful sculptural element in this work; indeed, one friend of mine who is most proficient in drawing lines and is also an amateur sculptor, tells me that the two activities give him much the same kind of satisfaction, and that he feels he is employing similar talents in either. The talent is not necessarily one that will produce a consistently reliable naval architect, any more than the skill with tools that may enable someone to carve the model of a hull out of a block of wood will assure that the model is the right shape for the ship's purpose. The person with the ability to produce a set of lines quickly and readily is the counterpart of the dextrous modeller, and working for precisely the same purpose – to express the shape of a solid form so that it may be reproduced at enlarged size. So the sculptural element in drawing hull-lines is not surprising.

Skill is required not only to draw hull-lines but to read them so as to get all that they are able to tell you from them. Month after month the yachting journals publish lines drawings, but many people are still unable to read them. Accommodation plans are little harder to understand than the plan of a house, though even these may lead amateurs into confusion owing to the fact that a hull, unlike a room, is curved in all directions and gets smaller as you go deeper into it. How often will the experienced suggest fitting a berth or a sideboard in a position that would in practice be half outside the skin of the hull, though it might appear inside the deckline of the layout drawing?

Lines take more understanding than layouts. Perhaps the best introduction to lines drawings may be found in yacht models, for modelling was the method of hull design that preceded drawing. The model method had the disadvantage of making difficult and clumsy, or completely impossible, many of the calculations that scientific design showed to be necessary, and which might be readily worked from a lines drawing. But the model had, and still has, some advantages over the drawing, and may be used today in design work as an adjunct to the drawing. A sheerline, for example, is a most difficult curve to develop satisfactorily on paper, for the distortions that this important line undergoes when reproduced in three dimensions cannot be easily assessed from a drawing. Architects may adjust this line on a model made from the lines drawing and transfer back to the drawing the revised sheer lifted from the model.

The models used for design work were generally of two kinds. The earliest was the simple half-model, which formed the shape of many early yachts. Such models were carved from a solid block of pine or mahogany by means of a drawknife, chisels, gouges, small planes, scrapers and finally sandpaper. The shape evolved was a matter of judgement; and we need not sniff at this. Where sailing yachts are concerned, judgement yesterday guided the chisel, today judgement and often nothing more guides the pencil, and there is nothing intrinsically more scientific about a pencil than a chisel. In a case like this they are just two tools for doing the same thing in different ways.

Having completed the half-model, the next task was to enlarge the shape it showed to full size and in a form that would be of use to the boatbuilder. One method was to mark on the top and keel of the model the positions of the frames, or alternate frames. A thin lead bar would then be bent round the model at each of the frames marked, and from the template of each frame so obtained their shapes might be traced on to paper, and offsets, according to the scale of the model, would be measured; from which the frames might be drawn out at full size on the loft floor.

This method was not considered very accurate, however. An alternative was to mount the half-model with the frame positions marked on it on to a blackboard; then to make fine saw cuts right across the model at each frame. Paper or thin card was then inserted into the cuts and the shape of the hull section at each position traced on to it. Then would follow the same process of enlargement to full size.

It was later, some time in the latter half of the eighteenth century, by which time lines drawings were being made for the bigger or more important ships, that what was known as the lift model was devised. One amongst many yachts designed by means of a lift model was the famous *America*, and the method, known in Britain as the 'bread-and-butter' system is often used today by ship modellers and the builders of model racing yachts; though for the latter the technique has to be elaborated.

The lift model was built not from a solid block but from a block formed of layers of timber screwed together, planks of a thickness that represented, according to the scale of the model, an easily measured distance at full size. When the carving of the model was completed, the lifts were unscrewed. The curve of each represented what, in a modern lines drawing, we describe as a *waterline* – this we will be discussing later – and each lift might be laid on paper and its shape traced.

From the various waterlines offsets might be measured enabling the sections or frames to be drawn at full size on the loft floor. (For the reader who cannot yet understand a set of lines this may not be clear, but it will be later.) The advantage of the lift model was its greater accuracy compared with the solid block model, the shape of which could only be enlarged by lead bar templates or saw cuts, both of which introduced errors.

So long as the creation of a hull shape is mainly governed by an instinctive appreciation of form, the model is better than any drawing. There are yacht architects working today who would do just as good work with a model if they were no less at home using chisels and planes than splines and pencils. The only calculations often made by yacht architects are of displacement and centre of buoyancy, both of which may be determined from the model by experimental methods.

Crude drawings are still in existence showing that some knowledge had been gained of how to project the shape of a ship's hull on paper by the middle of the seventeenth century. France, thanks to the work of her energetic Minister of Marine at this period, Jean Baptiste Colbert, led the world in scientific naval architecture. It is not surprising that in 1681, in the course of a series of conferences concerned with the problems of shipbuilding, one of those particularly studied was how to represent ship forms on paper by geometrical methods. By the early eighteenth century the best naval architects were able to produce well-drawn lines plans.

A modern yacht model made for test purposes in the Saunders-Roe test tank at Cowes is shown in Plate 13. This model has been built in wood on the lift principle, but the lifts are not the horizontal waterlines mentioned above but the vertical *buttock*-lines. We shall be referring to this picture again, for the manner of its construction and the clearly visible lifts will help to explain later some of the lines on a lines plan.

\*       \*       \*

In Fig. 1 we have a set of hull-lines of a small fishing-boat. Fig. 2 is a couple of isometric drawings of the same boat and showing the

same lines – sections, buttocks, waterlines – on this different projection. Isometric drawings are more immediately understand-
able to the uninitiated, but it seems to be their only merit. They
can reveal nothing that is not more exactly expressed in a set of
hull-lines, no calculations can be worked from them, and they are
useless for design purposes because they can be produced only
from a completed set of hull-lines.

Yet those naval architects with a love of fine draughtsmanship –
and there have been many particularly in the past – have been
attracted to the isometric representation of their designs, and some
lovely examples of such work appeared in a well-known folio of
designs published by the great Swedish-naturalized, British-born
architect Frederik Chapman nearly two hundred years ago. The
artistic work in this collection of ship designs is believed to have
been done by the Dutch artist Bogman, and there is something
pleasing, and lost today, in this treatment of ships' drawings as
works of art.

We must now consider nomenclature. There are three separate
drawings in Fig. 1. The top is known as the *body plan*, and it shows
what are known as the *sections* of the hull; and for this reason it
is nowadays often called the *section plan*. More precisely, they
should be called *cross-sections*, for the other curved lines on the
other plans are no less sections, though in other planes. But by
convention the term is reserved for the curved lines in the body
plan.

The middle plan is known as the *sheer plan* and sometimes nowadays the *elevation*. Its boundary-line is the profile of the hull as it
would appear in a cast shadow, or if the hull were sawn longi-
tudinally down its centreline. Apart from the straight lines, to
which we shall be returning later, there is a series of curved
lines numbered in Roman numerals i, ii, iii. These we now call
*buttocks*. Not long ago, and more logically, only the length of these
lines lying abaft amidships were called buttocks and their exten-
sions forward were named 'bow-lines', but now, at a cost of some
clarity often, the whole length of the lines usually receives the name
of buttock.

The bottom plan is known as the *half-breadth* drawing, or more casually the *waterline* plan. The boundary is a plan view of the deck (or if the hull at some point is broader above or below the deck than at it, the line at this level will run outside the deckline, as does the whaleback line in Fig. 1 and also the rail aft). As in the other two plans this drawing is composed of one set of curved lines while the others are straight, and the curved lines are known as *waterlines*.

Here again nomenclature has become simplified lately with a similar loss of clarity. Formerly the waterlines below a certain point designated as a datum waterline, which was the level at which under certain specified conditions the ship would float, were known as waterlines, while those running up into the topsides were called level lines. Now the term waterline is applied to both.

For the moment we will neglect the curved lines lying below the centreline of the hull in the half-breadth plan of Fig. 1. I want to say a word instead about the various straight lines on the three drawings. They are all based on the straight line labelled DWL on the body plan. What does this mean? Rash yacht architects may say it means 'designed waterline' but it is surprisingly unusual for a yacht to float in practice at the level shown on her drawings as her designated waterline.

It is, however, essential for purposes of design and calculation for an architect to assume that the vessel he is drawing will float at some level; so, as one of the first steps in making a drawing, he strikes more or less horizontally across a sheet of yet unravished drawing paper a straight line which expresses in its essence all the faith of a trusting bride. 'Here,' he says, 'this yacht will, under some conditions, have its waterline.'

By the time he has finished the design the conditions may belong to a different world from this, and the yacht may never in her life float at the level shown on the drawings. This might or might not have serious consequences in practice; so far as the construction of lines plans is concerned, it doesn't matter at all. We will rename the line concerned, as many yacht architects wisely do, datum waterline; it is the level at or near which we trust the yacht will float and from which all calculations will be made. Now I want to follow this datum waterline, labelled DWL on the body plan in Fig. 1, through the other two projections.

Apart from the baseline, one of the horizontal lines in the elevation plan is extended beyond the boundary of the hull profile. To our confusion it is labelled WL 4, and for this we will forgive the architect; it represents the same line as that labelled DWL in the body plan. It is the assumed line of flotation.

Move down farther to the half-breadth plan and you will see a curved line also labelled '4'. This is the straight DWL of the section and half-breadth drawings but represented in plan. It is the horizontal contour of the hull at that level. It will be seen that in the half-breadth drawing, equally spaced above and below WL or DWL other waterlines are shown, pecked above WL 4 and solid below it. Corresponding waterlines above and below the datum are likewise shown across the body plan; though here (we must forgive the architect again for his lack of consistency) he has drawn only one above DWL; correctly, the other two should appear. In the half-breadth plan, WLs 1 to 7, labelled as in the sheer plan, appear as curved contour lines, and they are precisely analogous to the contour lines of a map.

Any one set of contours is enough to define a solid shape. Given simply the half-breadth plan and the spacing between the waterlines, both the sheer plan and the body might be reconstructed without further information. But when creating *ab initio* a solid shape on paper more than one set of contours is needed to ensure that the shape is harmonious and suitable in all its planes. Also, to derive from a drawing a complete impression of what a hull is like, contours in several planes are needed, just as a model is viewed from several angles when judging its shape.

Another set of contours is the buttock-lines. We have already noted that these appear as curved on the sheer plan. The buttocks appear as straight lines in the half-breadth plan and numbered, i, ii, iii in correspondence with their labelling in the sheer plan. While the waterlines are contours in a longitudinal horizontal plane, buttocks are similar contours in a longitudinal vertical plane. The buttock labelled iii, for example, represents the outline shape of the hull were it cut vertically downwards parallel to the centreline and at the distance from it indicated by the position of buttock iii in the half-breadth drawing.

Buttocks are, as it were, vertical waterlines. The profile of the hull as indicated by the boundary-line of the sheer plan is, in effect, a buttock-line at the fore and aft central plane of the hull. The buttock-lines should also appear as straight lines on either side of the centreline of the body plan, but for no good reason they have been omitted in Fig. 1.

Unlike waterlines and buttock-lines, sections are generally promptly understood even by laymen. They are transverse sections through the hull at a number of points. They are represented by the straight, vertical lines numbered 0 to 10 on the sheer and half-breadth drawings, these lines showing the positions of the sections whose actual shapes appear in the body plan, where they are numbered in the same way.

We may summarize thus: sections, waterlines and buttocks are the shapes that would appear were a hull sawn through along different planes; sections are the shapes that appear when the cuts are made vertically and across the model; waterlines are lengthwise horizontal cuts; buttocks lengthwise vertical cuts. Each set of cuts appears in all three of the projections, in two of them as straight lines indicating position and in the third of curves indicating shape. Thus:

|            | Body Plan | Sheer    | Half-breadth |
|------------|-----------|----------|--------------|
| Sections   | curved    | straight | straight     |
| Waterlines | straight  | straight | curved       |
| Buttocks   | straight  | curved   | straight     |

\*       \*       \*

I should like to consider now for a moment a little more closely than earlier how the various projections in the body plan, sheer plan and half-breadth drawing are lined together.

Turn to the *sheer plan* in Fig. 1, in which the buttocks are the curved lines, and look at the section numbered 8. By an odd chance it happens that the straight, vertical line of the section at 8, the three horizontal straight lines labelled respectively WL 2, 4 and 6, and the curved buttock-lines labelled I, II, and III almost precisely intersect one another. Now follow those lines, again at section 8, down to the half-breadth plan and you will find similar intersections, though in this drawing it is the waterlines that are curved. That is, when we find, for example, in the sheer plan that buttock III and WL 2 intersect precisely at section 8, we find the same occurring in the half-breadth plan. If this were not so it would mean that the two drawings showed different shapes.

Even in refined modern yacht architecture, drawings do sometimes show different shapes between one projection and another. Nothing being perfect in this world, it is impossible to produce a perfectly fair set of hull-lines; but some are more unfair than others. Then everything depends on the boatbuilder. The architect may show three slightly different boats in his three different drawings of the set of lines; but unless the builder produces three boats, instead of the one for which the contract was drawn, he has to strike a mean. The fact that timber bends naturally into fair curves and is difficult to distort produces some sort of reconciliation between inadequately faired drawings.

I will not enlarge on this further. If, with schoolboy knowledge of map contours, the hull-lines of Fig. 1 and the isometric drawing of Fig. 2 are compared, the relationship between the various lines will be understood. Look at the bow view of the isometric drawing. You will find the same intersections between buttock, section and waterline as those shown in the lines plan; you will find the same intersection at section 8 (though it is not labelled such) of the outer buttock (I) and the DWL or WL 4, as it is variously named in the lines plan. (The DWL in the isometric drawing has been traced more heavily than the other waterlines.)

Still unmentioned are the curved lines at the bottom of Fig. 1, labelled A, B, C and D, but unfortunately not shown on the body plan, the diagonals. We have said earlier that *sections* are transverse vertical contours, *buttock* longitudinal vertical contours, *waterlines* horizontal longitudinal contours. *Diagonals* are diagonal longitudinal contours. Why, for Pete's sake, have any more contours, it

may be wondered, having already taken them in the three dimensions that make a solid?

Diagonals happen to be the most valuable fairing-lines at a
draughtsman's disposal. If you examine the diagonals in a yacht's
body plan where they appear as straight lines, you will see that
they cross the curved sections everywhere as nearly as possible at a
right angle. Every navigator knows that when taking a cross
bearing fix it is desirable that the two position lines should cross one
another as nearly at right angles as possible. If the angle is small
the point of intersection of the two pencil lines on the chart is
indefinite, and an error in bearing of a few degrees will produce a
big error in position, which is not the case if the intersection is
close to the normal.

The navigator at the chart table and the architect at the drawing-
table is faced with the same problem. For the highest accuracy,
intersecting lines should cut nearly at right angles. Buttock-lines
in the sheer plan in the amidships region tend to make bad cuts
with the waterlines; waterlines in the half-breadth plan tend to
make bad cuts with the buttocks-lines. But suitably arranged
diagonals across the body plan may make good cuts with all the
sections. When the ship modeller is finely fairing the model with
glass paper he runs his fingertips over the surface to detect in-
equalities. The fingers are most sensitive instruments for this
purpose and able to detect otherwise invisible unfairnesses; but
the draughtsman cannot use his fingertips on a drawing; diagonals
are their substitute.

There are some architects who do almost all the fairing with
diagonals – Knud Reimers is a notable example. Robert Clark
uses an impressive number of diagonals to ensure the fairness of a
set of lines and to provide a greater number of offset measurements
for laying-off full size. There are some designers who maintain
that, since waterlines are horizontal and buttock-lines vertical, the
diagonals should all be parallel and at 45 degrees. This makes a
drawing look neat for the diagonals, when laid off as curves below
the half-breadths, are all harmonious curves one inside the other.
But this system does destroy some of the valuable flexibility.
We do not know the position on the body plan of the diagonals in

Fig. 1, but it will be seen that when laid off as curves some of the lines cross one another. There is no significance in this; it is the outcome, in the present example, of diagonals A and B being drawn at different angles.

Architects have various ideas as to how many waterlines, buttocks and sections should be used when producing a lines drawing. A commonly adopted convention has established that the designed waterline (DWL) should be divided into ten equal parts by the sections, which has been done in Fig. 1. A usual practice, which has also been followed here, is that intermediate sections are drawn at the extremities of the hull where curvatures at bow and stern are acute; the intermediate sections are shown as pecked lines.

There is more diversity about the number of waterlines chosen. I have a drawing by me by Francis Jones, a most exact draughts-man, on which no fewer than 22 waterlines are shown – three times as many as in Fig. 1. He also plots seven diagonals and five buttocks.

\*　　　\*　　　\*

It was mentioned that the crucial feature of a lines drawing is that each of the views – the sheer plan, body plan and half-breadths – must not only be composed of fair curves laid over the grid of straight lines, but that each plan should represent the same shape, and that this occurs when the various intersections of the curves and straight lines in the three projections correspond one with the other.

Reverting to Fig. 1 we see that on the sheer plan the inner buttock labelled III intersects the waterline labelled WL 2 almost precisely at section 8. Now turning to the waterline plan, we may observe with relief that WL 2 hardly less precisely crosses with the intersection of the straight lines representing, in this projection, the above waterline and buttock. If it did not do so, it would become a question poised between the shipwright, his god and his timber what precise shape the hull assumed in this locality. And since, where long sweet curves are concerned, abrupt changes are impossible and inaccuracies move with smooth inevitability along the flowing lines, a lines drawing inaccurate in one place will be so in others.

The major error at section 5, for example, will still be present, if less considerable, at sections 6 and 7. It is like the sins of the fathers visiting themselves on all those luckless future generations. If, say, a waterline and buttock intersection is inaccurate on the half-breadth drawing, the curve of the waterline will have to be adjusted. Not only will the adjustment run over into the neighbouring section and buttock-lines, but the corresponding lines will have to be adjusted in each of the other plans, and to fair a curve in one plan may need adjustments in as many as ten places on the various projections.

And if the spacings of the various lines is halved the number of corrections to be made will be doubled, and the architect will get into such a tizzy in the process that nothing will in the end be better than if he had assured the accuracy with fewer fairing-lines. But if the lines are to be finally traced for reproduction, then closely spaced waterlines and buttock do offer a more attractive and easily visualized impression of the solid form, and for this aesthetic purpose the additional lines may be plotted.

Here we might mention some of the many conventions usually adopted in drawing lines plans. Most architects nowadays show the bow to the right-hand side of the paper. A few, with a flourish of independence, do the reverse, and once this was more common than it is now. According to Francis Herreschoff, 'this custom came from making a model first with the stations laid off on its centre-lines from left to right, but when the model was turned over and laid on the drawing (to draw the pencil around to get the sheer and profile) then the station numbers read from right to left'. This is not clear to me; but it would not be surprising to find a drawing convention originating in the model-making days.

It might seem a purely arbitrary matter, which side to place the bow, but I believe it has a discernible influence on design. Hold any drawing up to a looking glass and notice how different the profile appears when reversed; the sheerline undergoes the strange transformation of becoming more exaggerated when the bow appears to the left, and other straight lines and curves alter their relationships to one another.

I have already said that it is customary for the datum waterline to be divided into ten equal parts by the sections of the body plan. Some architects will maintain that more sections than this are required for adequate fairing; and when a design is to be tank tested closer spacing is necessary in order to ensure the required accuracy in the calculations. But ten sections will often suffice.

There is another consideration that should (but rarely, it seems, does nowadays) affect either the section spacing or the length chosen for the DWL, and that is the convenience of the loftsman who is going to lay the design off full size using, probably, a rule graduated in eighths of an inch. With ten section spaces, datum waterlines of 25 ft, 30 ft and 35 ft are convenient for they give spacings of 2 ft 6 in, 3 ft 0 in. and 3 ft 6 in. respectively. The popular 24-ft waterline encouraged by the RORC rule is an unhappy length when divided by ten, for the nearest approach to one-tenth of this measurement on an eighth-inch rule is 2 ft 4$\frac{3}{4}$ in. and there will be an error of half an inch in the laid length of the datum waterline if this figure is used.

With a 24-ft waterline there is an obvious argument for using twelve section spaces. When there is no reason to adopt a tidy looking figure for length of waterline, it is more reasonable to adopt, say, 25 ft 5 in. rather than 25 ft 6 in., for one-tenth of the former is 2 ft 6$\frac{1}{2}$ in., and of the latter it is fractionally more than 2 ft 6$\frac{19}{32}$ in. It should perhaps be added here, though most people will know the fact, that lines are now drawn to the outside of the planking, and after laying off the lines a loftsman has to deduct planking thickness in order to obtain the mould sizes. In all early lines drawings the lines were drawn moulded, or to the inside of the planking, a great convenience to builders.

Several other differences will be found in early drawings. We have seen that today the basis of a drawing is the datum waterline. But when ships had long, straight keels it used to be the line of the keel which formed the horizontal base line. Once afloat most of the smaller vessels drawn thus had, in fact, considerable drag to the bottom of the keel – the keel sloped downwards from the stem

K*

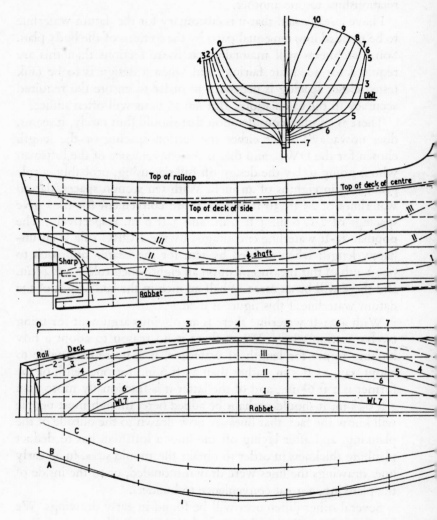

FIG. I. Lines of a small fishing fessel. *Top:* The body plan. *Centre* plan or elevation. *Bottom:* The half-breadth plan.

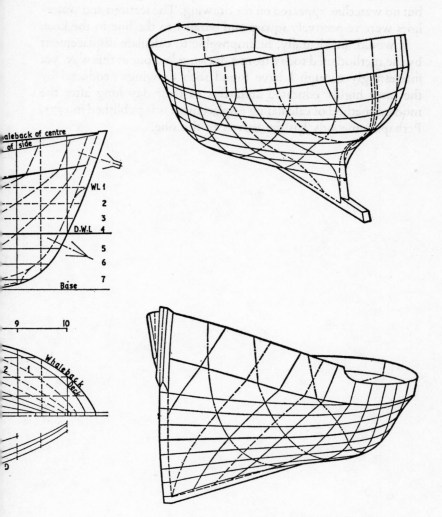

to the back of the cradle system. On the top of the cradle was a raised
bar no wreckage appeared on the railway. The scenes and water
lines were so curved, square section ... table line ... the lower

FIG. 2. Isometric drawings from bow to stern
of small fishing vessel shown in Fig. 1.

to the heel of the rudder, where the deepest draught was situated – but no waterline appeared on the drawing. The sections and water-lines were respectively square and parallel to the line to the keel.

It would, incidentally, be impossible to calculate displacement by the method used today from a drawing laid out in this way, yet interestingly enough I have found such drawings produced by the most highly educated architects of their day long after the modern method of calculating displacement was published in 1775. Perhaps somebody has the answer to this one.

# INDEX OF SUBJECTS

# INDEX OF YACHTS